FLOWERS
FOR
CELEBRATIONS

FLOWERS
FOR
CELEBRATIONS

MING VEEVERS-CARTER

MEREHURST

LONDON

To Topher Faulkner, for his
constant love and support

Published 1989 by Merehurst Limited
Ferry House,
51-57 Lacy Road
Putney
London SW15 1PR

© Copyright 1989 Merehurst Limited
Reprinted 1991

ISBN 1-85391-025-2 (Cased)
ISBN 1-85391-176-3 (Paperback)

Edited by Jane Struthers
Designed by Peartree Design Associates
Photographed by Jon Stewart, assisted by Alister Thorpe
Styling by Barbara Stewart
Typeset by Rowland Phototypesetting Limited,
Bury St Edmunds, Suffolk
Colour separation by Fotographics Limited,
London – Hong Kong
Printed in Italy by New Interlitho S.p.A., Milan

CONTENTS

FOREWORD

Of all the expressions of joy, flowers are the purest and most perfect. There is no better way to celebrate all our important occasions, and from the dawn of civilisation man has used flowers to express his supremely personal emotions. Flowers are the most natural way to celebrate as they are themselves nature's perfect celebration. Whether it is to decorate our homes, welcome a new baby, congratulate, praise, woo or wed, the giving and receiving of flowers will always be the most spontaneous way with which to show our feelings. Of all the rites of passage, the celebration of marriage perhaps holds the greatest beauty. The image of the radiant bride is closely linked to the flowers she chooses for her wedding day, be they for her bouquet, her head dress, to decorate the church or the reception. On this day she will choose her flowers with the greatest attention to every detail, scent and colour as a memory to treasure in the future, for at any wedding it is the flowers which reflect the exaltation of the occasion, whether it be a royal wedding watched by millions or a country wedding in the local church. From the smallest bridesmaid to the bride's mother, all wear their flowers as a symbol of joy and happiness.

In this, her first book, Ming Veevers-Carter shares with us her love of plants, her skill and experience at choosing and selecting the right flowers for the occasion and her enthusiasm for the art of celebration flowers. Above all, she shows how to use the flowers to reflect the delights of celebration using nature's most perfect creation.

SANDRA BOLER
Editor, Bride's Magazine

Techniques and Equipment

The secret of a successful flower arrangement lies primarily in the way it is constructed, and if you have never used wire netting or oasis when arranging flowers you will be astonished at the difference they make. In this section of the book I will be demonstrating a range of useful floristry techniques, with the help of clear step-by-step photographs and captions.

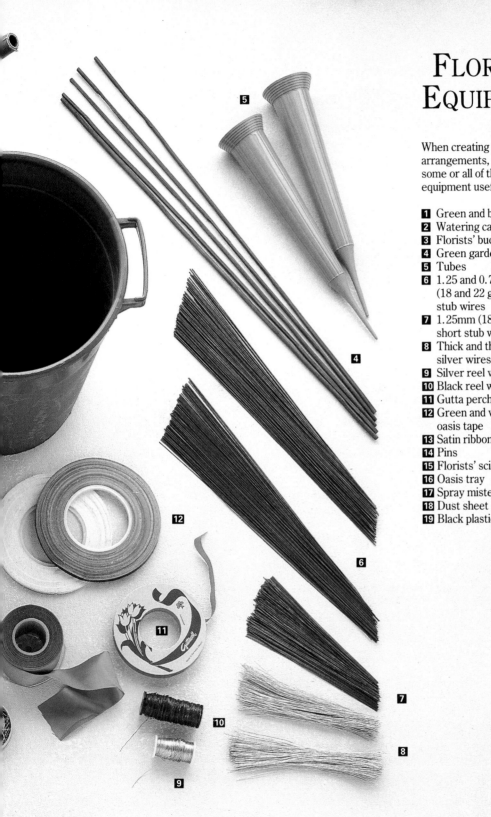

FLORISTS' EQUIPMENT

When creating your own arrangements, you may find some or all of the following equipment useful:

1. Green and brown oasis
2. Watering can
3. Florists' bucket
4. Green garden sticks
5. Tubes
6. 1.25 and 0.71mm (18 and 22 gauge) stub wires
7. 1.25mm (18 gauge) short stub wires
8. Thick and thin silver wires
9. Silver reel wire
10. Black reel wire
11. Gutta percha
12. Green and white oasis tape
13. Satin ribbon
14. Pins
15. Florists' scissors
16. Oasis tray
17. Spray mister
18. Dust sheet
19. Black plastic bag

WIRING FLOWERS AND FOLIAGE

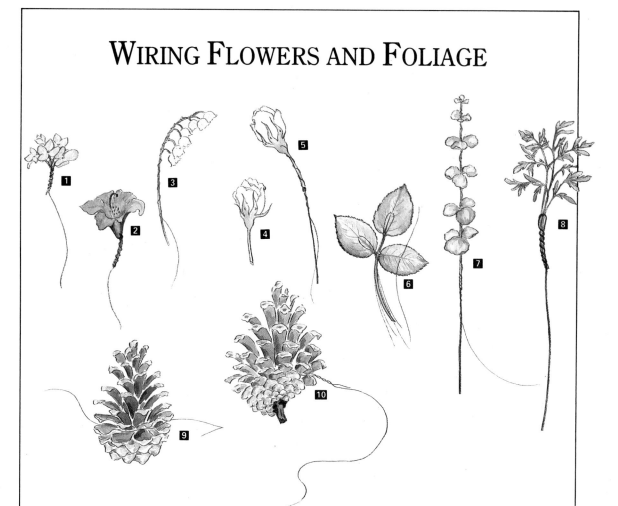

1 When wiring such flowers as hydrangea florets, wire them as close to the top of the floret as possible to stop them drooping.

2 If wiring a single flower, such as a rhododendron flower, insert a thick silver wire through the base of the flower and twist the ends around the stem. If using such a flower for a wedding bouquet, you should push a 1.25mm (18 gauge) or 0.71mm (22 gauge) silver wire up the stem first.

3 For flowers that bear many bells on a thin stem, such as lily of the valley, use the thinnest silver wire and make a small loop around the top bell, then wind the ends down between each remaining bell. Unless the flower is being used for a head dress you should first push a 0.71mm (22 gauge) wire up the stem.

4 When using roses in a bouquet, head dress or buttonhole, you should pin the calyx to the petals with tiny silver wire pins.

5 To wire the rest of the rose, push a 1.25mm (18 gauge) wire up the stem, holding it in place by inserting a thick silver wire into the base of the flower and twisting the end down the stem.

6 When wiring rose leaves for buttonholes, choose a stem bearing three leaves that are in perfect condition. Starting with the top leaf, thread a thin silver wire about halfway through

the back, bend and twist the wires down to the end of the stem. Repeat with the other two leaves. This will enable you to arrange the leaves in precisely the position you require and will stop them drooping.

7 If wiring longer stems of foliage, such as ivy or other trailing foliage, insert a 0.71mm (22 gauge) wire up the stem, then wire the leaves with thin silver wire, starting at the top and twisting it all the way down the stem.

8 When using a harder foliage such as rue, senecio or pittosporum, rest the leaves in the palm of your hand, with the stems between your thumb and forefinger. Place the 0.71mm (22 gauge) wire across the stems then fold it down towards the end of the stems, so that one piece of wire is only just longer than the stems. Taking the longest wire, twist tightly until you reach the end of the stem.

9 When wiring an opened pine cone for an arrangement, thread a 1.25mm (18 gauge) stub wire around the cone, ensuring that it goes in as deeply as possible. Use a 0.71mm (22 gauge) stub for a garland.

10 Pull the two ends together and twist well. Hold the wire about 5cm (2in) from the twist and pull downwards.

Conditioning Flowers and Foliage

1 When using such flowers as irises, tulips, lilies, daffodils and other soft-stemmed flowers, always cut the stems at an angle of 45° before placing them in water.

2 Roses are almost the only hardwood stemmed flowers that are split rather than bashed with a hammer. Using a sharp pair of scissors, make a cut up the stem about 4cm (1½ in) long, having first cut the stem at an angle of 45°.

3 For all other hardwood flowers and foliage, nigella and lily of the valley, you should hammer the stems. Cut the stem at a 45° angle, place the flower on a concrete floor or block of wood and

hammer the bottom of the stem well, without reducing it to a pulp!

4 You must boil the stems of such plants as lilac, cow parsley, euphorbias, dill, moluccella, artichoke leaves and any plant that has a drooping head or leaves, hydrangeas being a typical example. To do this, fill a bucket with between 10–15cm (4–6in) boiling water, then cut the stems at a 45° angle and hammer them. Leave the stems in the water for at least 10 minutes. If you will not be using them the same day, either leave the flowers in the bucket or place them in fresh water until needed.

Making a Wedding Bouquet and Posy

1 Choose pretty and delicate foliage, then cut it down to pieces about 10cm (4in) long. For a trailing bouquet, use 17.5-cm (7-in) lengths of jasmine, ivy, honeysuckle or similar plants. Wire the flowers that will be used at the base of the trailing bouquet, as well as any heavy flowers such as hyacinths, large roses or lilies, with 1.25mm (18 gauge) stub wires. Use 0.71mm (22 gauge) wires for the other items. Cover the foliage and flower wires with gutta percha.

2 Gather together about 10 stems of foliage so that the tops are roughly level. Bind together with silver reel wire very firmly, wrapping it around the stems about six times. This stage is very important as it forms the main construction for the bouquet or posy. Do not cut the reel wire as it will be easier to handle if kept on the roll.

3 Holding the wires firmly in your hand, gently pull outwards about five pieces of foliage to make a circle, and arrange the others to fill in the gaps from the top to the sides. Wrap the wire around twice more, for safety. The wire must be wound around the same part of the stems throughout, or the bouquet will lose its shape.

4 To make a trailing bouquet, follow steps 1, 2 and 3, then add the trailing foliage to one side of the circle to create a soft and gentle flow. At this stage you may wish to enlarge the original circle by placing a wired piece of foliage flat against the circle, wiring it in and then shaping it.

5 When adding flowers to the posy, insert them through the foliage one at a time. Once each flower is in position, wrap the reel wire round the stems to hold it in place before adding the next flower. Every time you add anything to the bouquet, you must bind it firmly in position with reel wire.

6 Once you have added all the flowers and foliage, secure the reel wire before cutting it off by threading it through the guttared wire stems and pulling it upwards. Then, trim off the stems to make a thinner handle for the bouquet. Make sure you cut them no closer than 5cm (2in) from the reel wire, and trim the wires so that they graduate to a point.

7 Now wrap the silver reel wire down over the handle to hold the wires in place, then cover the handle with gutta percha, working from the top of the handle down to the point. It is best to wrap it round with gutta twice to prevent any wires poking through.

8 Bend the handle into a curved shape. Using 12-mm (2-in) satin ribbon, fold the top corner of the ribbon over, place this at the top of the handle and pin into place, pushing the pin upwards to avoid accidents. This will hold the ribbon in place, then wrap it tightly all the way down the handle and back up, securing it in the same way as before. Tie off with a bow (see steps 5 and 6 on pages 16–17).

Making a Head Dress, Comb and Half Circlet

1 You will gain maximum effect if you use a variety of shapes as well as colours when making a head dress, so try to choose at least five different types each of flowers and foliage and wire them all individually. Here, I used muscari, gypsophila, tea roses, moluccella, ranunculus, laurustinus, pussy willow, variegated ivy and peperomia leaves.

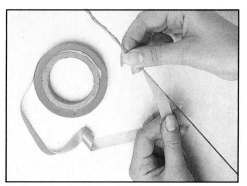

2 To make the circlet, bind together two lengths of 1.25mm (18 gauge) wire, then cover them with gutta percha.

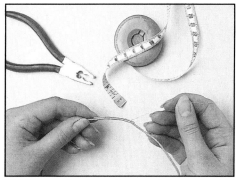

3 Measure the circumference of the head, add an extra 10cm (4in) for the overlap, then cut the wires to the appropriate length. Curve into a hoop, overlapping the two wires until the circle is the desired size, and firmly bind the ends together with silver wire. Cover the join with gutta percha.

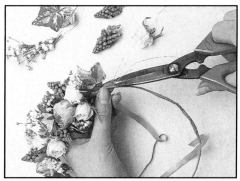

4 Starting with an ivy leaf, place it flat on the hoop. Twist the wire around the hoop four or five times, then cut off any excess. Using gutta percha cut to half its normal width, bind the wire to the hoop. Continue working around the hoop in this way until you have wired all the flowers and foliage in place, leaving a gap of 2.5cm (1in) at the back.

5 Taking a length of ribbon in your hand, form it into a neat bow. Bind the centre tightly with silver wire and trim off any excess.

6 Tie a length of ribbon, about 50cm (20in), in the gap left at the back of the circlet, then place the bow on top of the knot and tie again to secure it in place.

7 Follow the instructions for steps 1, 2 and 4 when making a comb, but each time bring the wire and gutta percha through the teeth of the comb.

8 The same principles shown in step 4 apply when making a half circlet or band, except that you must bend the ends of the main wire together, bind them with silver wire and then cover with gutta percha. Work from the ends of the wire towards the middle, ensuring that this is the highest point.

MAKING A DECORATED BASKET

1 Choose a basket that is the right size for the person carrying it. Wire all the flowers and foliage as for a head dress (*see pp 16–17*), then cover the wires with white or green gutta percha. The flowers used here are roses, laurustinus and hydrangea florets. When using hydrangeas, make sure you wire them very close to the flowers or they will droop.

2 Measure one side of the basket and then, beginning with a rose, entwine the stems of the flowers and foliage together, ensuring that you also end the garland with a rose.

3 Place the garland of flowers around the rim of the basket. Fasten it in position with thin silver wires – securing both ends of the garland and its centre should be adequate.

4 Repeat steps 2 and 3 to make the garland for the other half of the basket rim. You can provide an attractive finishing touch by winding some satin ribbon around the handle, tying two bows where the handle joins the basket. The basket can be filled with confetti or rose petals.

DECORATING THE ENTRANCE TO A MARQUEE

1 Wrap half a block of wet oasis in wire netting, making sure it is secure by twisting together the opposite ends of the netting. Thread a 1.25mm (18 gauge) wire through the top of the oasis block and pull and twist together to make a loop, then using double lengths of black reel wire, attach the oasis to the frame of the marquee.

2 Using a mixture of foliage – at least three types – loosely fill in the basic shape. If the arrangement does not look pleasing to the eye at this stage, then it is unlikely to do so later on. You must therefore be happy with this stage before moving on to the next.

3 Add the thickest and heaviest flowers first, again making sure you like the effect. Do not put all the flowers just on the outer edge, but place a few in the middle so that the arrangement flows.

4 Next add the forsythia, then the double pink tulips, blue bee and finally the roses. Do not try to overfill the arrangement, especially of this type, as the oasis simply will not hold. To ensure the flowers stay fresh, spray very frequently and keep the oasis wet.

DECORATING A MARQUEE POLE

1 Wrap three three-quarter blocks of wet oasis as shown in step 1 on page 19. Line the backs with plastic pinned on to the oasis with 7.5cm (3in) wire pins. Fix three screws around the pole, evenly spaced, and three beneath them, as shown in the photograph. Wire the blocks of oasis to the top and bottom nails, then wire the blocks together with 0.71mm (22 gauge) wire.

2 If you are using blossom, place this into the oasis first as the stems are very thick and heavy and will easily form a pretty shape from which to work. The difficulty in decorating a pole is that one has to keep moving the ladder around to create an even, all-round arrangement.

3 Add the rest of the foliage, filling in the spaces left by the blossom. I cannot stress enough how important it is that an arrangement should look pleasing at every stage, so do not progress from one step to the next until you are satisfied with your work.

4 Before you put any stem into the arrangement, look at its shape and the way it naturally falls, remembering that it will be seen from below. Consider all these factors before arranging the flowers and foliage, since if you keep inserting and removing the stems from the oasis block, it will soon disintegrate and you will have to start all over again.

5 Look carefully at steps 3 and 4, to see how the shape has grown and filled out without looking overcrowded. Now that the foliage is virtually an arrangement on its own, you can add the flowers – arrange the lilies first, then the blue bee and finally the roses.

6 An alternative to a large arrangement is just to cover the pole with pretty trails of ivy, by gently pinning the pieces to the pole cloth. When choosing the ivy, make sure that it is not a thick, stiff, ugly and unmanageable variety, as this arrangement must look delicate and natural, not heavy and forced.

7 You can also make small arrangements based on the same principle as one large one, but using quarter blocks of oasis instead of three-quarter blocks. Most marquee pole cloths are straight, so to create this ruched effect you will have to line the pole yourself. When you hammer the nails into place, gather up the cloth first, then position it around the finished arrangement. The flowers and foliage used here are *Euphorbia marginata*, ranunculus, 'Lovely Girl' roses and white blossom.

8 To create these flower garlands, cut a block of oasis in half lengthways, then into four widthways to give eight pieces. Cut a strip of netting about 15cm (6in) wide and long enough to twine around the width of the marquee pole. Line the oasis up along the length of the netting and wrap. Hammer a nail into the top of the pole, attach one end of the oasis netting tube and then wrap around the pole. Starting at the top, place the foliage all the way down the tube, then add the flowers to give a uniform effect. In this garland we used hellebores, maidenhair fern, parrot tulips, 'Lovely Girl' roses and muscari.

MAKING TABLE SWAGS

1 For this posy, I used a mixture of lavender, 'Porcelain' roses, 'Evelyn' spray roses, rue and hebe foliage.

2 Gather together about eight pieces of rue and hebe in your hand and wire them to make a pleasing all-round shape (*see p 27*). Add the 'Porcelain' roses and wrap the wire round, then wire in the 'Evelyn' roses and finally the lavender. This follows the principle of always adding add the largest flowers first and graduating to the smallest.

3 Once all the flowers and foliage are securely wired and the effect is pleasing to the eye, cut off the stems to make a handle about 5cm (2in) long. Tie on the satin bow (*see p 28*).

4 Placing the posy so that it faces outwards from the edge of the table where the swags of either fabric or foliage meet, place pins through the sides of the posy and straight down into the tablecloth. You will need about four pins for each posy, although you can sew the posies into position if necessary.

MAKING A CAKE TOP

1 Using a knife, trim a quarter block of wet oasis into a cone shape, then wrap the bottom of the cone in plastic and secure it with pins. When choosing the flowers, remember to keep them small and light. Here, we used trichilium, euphorbia, eucalyptus tips, blossom, muscari, ranunculus and *Senecio biocolor* 'Silver Dust'.

2 Gently place the foliage in the cone, making sure that it is evenly spaced all round, not too large, and that it is securely in position. Do not overfill with foliage at this stage, as you can always add more later.

3 Now add the ranunculus, as they are the largest and heaviest of the flowers. They also have very soft stems, so hold them close to the bottom of the stems when inserting them in the oasis to avoid breakages. Then add the muscari, handling it in the same way.

4 Then add the trichilium and blossom, water the oasis well from the top and spray. Leave it for about half an hour before placing on top of the cake, making sure that the bottom is dry.

MAKING A PEDESTAL WITH AND WITHOUT OASIS

1 When using just wire netting to support the flowers and foliage in a pedestal, cut a long strip of wire netting, place on a flat surface and roll into a dense but not tight ball. Keep turning the ball from side to side as you roll. When in position, the netting should sit about 10–12.5cm (4–5in) above the rim of the bowl.

2 When using oasis to support the flowers and foliage in a pedestal arrangement, soak three blocks of oasis in water, then place one across the bottom of the chosen bowl and two at right angles on top, as shown in the photograph.

3 Normally when using oasis, you can hold it in place with oasis tape, but that would be unsafe for a large arrangement such as this. Instead, roll up a small ball of wire netting, place it on top of the oasis and anchor firmly on opposite sides by securing one end of the black reel wire to the wire netting, passing the wire under the bowl and fixing it on the other side. Pull sharply so that the netting is flush with the bowl. Repeat on the other sides, twisting the wire around the first wire beneath the bowl. This also applies to the arrangement with just wire netting.

4 Quite often, when creating a large arrangement, not enough tall foliage and flowers are available, and tubes have to be used to increase the height of the existing material. Sometimes the height of the tubes will be adequate, but if not you can extend them by wiring green garden or bamboo sticks to the sides of the tubes.

5 Position the tubes in the arrangement before adding the flowers and foliage, as you will find it difficult to insert them afterwards. Make sure that they are firm and not wobbly before you start, as this precaution will save you a lot of trouble later on. To be really safe, extend each tube with two sticks.

6 Using the longest pieces of foliage, make your basic shape around the outside, through the middle and down over the front. Here, I used long eucalyptus. It is always better to create an arrangement of this size *in situ*, as you will be able to judge how high and how wide the arrangement should be, according to its surroundings.

7 Fill in the rest of the shape with foliage, arranging it lightly around the edges and making it denser towards the centre. The foliage should now hide 90 per cent of the mechanics. Here, I used camellia, pittosporum and laurustinus.

8 The amaryllis should be inserted next, because of the thickness of their stems. They should really be placed in the tubes, as the wire netting will only split their stems. Then I added lilac, cow parsley and finally the longiflorum lilies.

MAKING A FOOT CORSAGE

1 You will not need many flowers to make a foot corsage, but the ones you do choose should be small and delicate. Using 30cm (6in) lengths of silver wire, wire all the leaves and flowers individually, then bind each wire with gutta percha. I used white gutta percha because it looks better on a pale shoe.

2 For the base of the foot corsage, take a 12.5cm (5in) length of 1.25mm (18 gauge) wire and cover in white gutta percha. Assemble the flowers and foliage together in your hand, then twist the wires on to the base wire and bind firmly with the white gutta percha. Ensure that the ends of the wires are completely covered for maximum comfort.

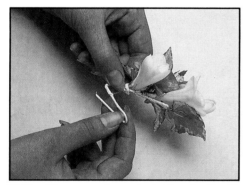

3 Bend the excess base wire back on itself until it resembles the shape of a paper clip.

4 Slide the corsage on to the shoe, anchoring it in position with the bent wire. If the shoes are to be worn for a long period, they will be more comfortable if you sew the corsages into place with a strong needle and thick button thread.

MAKING A TIED POSY

1 Starting with two stems of foliage (here I have used rosemary), cross the stems and bind them together with white or green gutta percha, making sure it is secure.

2 Keep adding the foliage. As you add more, continue to cross the stems and bind them with gutta. This is the only time in flower arranging that your stems should cross, as this will make the posy fan out.

3 Feed the flowers through from the top of the posy, also crossing the stems and binding them. In this posy I have used 'Porcelain' roses, white freesias, coral spray roses, laurustinus and rosemary.

4 Tie off the gutta percha by feeding it through the stems and pulling tightly. Cut off the stems evenly. The posy should be able to stand up on its own if you have crossed enough stems. Also, if you do not cross the stems you will find that the flowers will be crushed together in the centre of the posy and not evenly spaced. For a finishing touch, tie with satin ribbon.

MAKING A PLANTED BASKET

1 If the basket does not have its own waterproof lining, it should be lined with thick plastic sheeting. Fill it about half-full with good-quality potting compost.

2 Remove the plants from their plastic pots and arrange in the basket. Here I used 'Cheer' narcissi, jonquils, polyanthuses, helxene, jasmine and trailing ivy.

3 Once your plants are in position, fill in the gaps between their root balls with soil, making sure that they are all covered and firm. Do not fill the basket to the brim with soil as you will have trouble watering it – leave at least 2.5cm (1in) from the top of the basket. Trim off any excess plastic, leaving about 2.5cm (1in) above the top of the basket.

4 For the finishing touches use bun moss and pebbles or bark. When placing the moss on the edge of the basket, ensure that the excess plastic is folded outwards. This catches any water that might otherwise drip on to a table top. Between waterings, keep the plants moist by spraying them with water.

MAKING AN ARCHWAY

1 When choosing the branches for an archway you should first decide on the height and shape of the finished arch. You will find it much easier to use branches that are naturally bent rather than try to coax straight branches into curves. Once you have found suitable branches, place their bases in tubs of nylon reinforced plaster and leave to set for at least 24 hours.

2 Cut a strip of wire netting about 15cm (6in) wide and 1.2m (4ft) long, then cut a block of wet oasis into eight pieces and arrange them along the netting, separated by gaps of 5cm (2in). Wrap the netting around them to form a roll and secure the ends together firmly. Then place the roll on a branch and wire securely in place. Make as many of these oasis rolls as you need to attach them all round the archway.

3 Starting at the centre of the arch, begin to arrange the flowers and work down one side before beginning the other. In this arch I used wild gypsophila, white campanulas, Doris pinks, *Alchemilla mollis* and lavender sweet peas.

4 When you have finished decorating the sides of the arch, place a block of wet oasis into the bottom of each container and arrange greenery in it. Here, I used blue thistles, grasses and ferns to soften the bottom of the arch and the top of the container. The flowers will keep fresh if frequently sprayed, but the arrangement will not last for much more than a day.

MAKING A FACING ARRANGEMENT

1 Look closely at the way in which the stems all point towards the centre of the bowl in this photograph – when I talk about the central point in an arrangement, this is what I mean. As this is a facing arrangement, the foliage starts approximately three-quarters of the way back in the bowl.

2 Add more foliage – in this case, I used moluccella. When working with foliage of this type it is important to position it near the beginning of the arrangement as it has such dominant shapes.

3 Then add the ferns to fill in the outline, followed by *Euphorbia marginata*, to fill in the centre of the arrangement. Look at the different shapes and textures of the foliage used – the greater the variety, the more interesting the arrangement will be.

4 If you are using flowers with weak yet thick stems, such as the hyacinths shown here, position them after the foliage. As they are also relatively short they can be used to give a focal point to the arrangement. You can then add other flowers as you wish.

MAKING AN OVAL OR
ROUND ARRANGEMENT

1 I used oasis here because I was not going to work with any soft-stemmed foliage. When fitting oasis into a small bowl, you should leave enough room around the sides of the bowl to allow for water. Tape the oasis in place, and use the cross of the oasis tape as the central point. Make the basic shape with the foliage for a round arrangement.

2 To make an oval table arrangement, follow step 1 but add longer pieces of foliage at each end and graduate them gently into the circle, both sideways and upwards.

3 Start adding the flowers, keeping the outline within that of the foliage. Remember that this round arrangement will be seen mostly from the side, so make sure the rim of the bowl is completely covered with foliage and flowers. The flowers used here are white freesias.

4 You may find it easier to see the basic shape of the oval arrangement now that some of the flowers are in position. When arranging the flowers, do not leave a piece of flower or foliage languishing on its own, as this will give a pointed effect. Now add the rest of the flowers.

MAKING TOPIARY

1 Find an interesting piece of wood, about 1m (3ft) long, to use as the tree trunk. Set this into a flowerpot filled with nylon reinforced clay or plaster of Paris. Once it is set hard, hammer three nails into the stem about 5cm (2in) from the top and another about 15cm (6in) further down, spacing them evenly and at right angles to the trunk. They will hold the oasis in place.

2 Cut one block of oasis into four even pieces, then tightly wrap three of them in wire netting. Secure these pieces of oasis to the trunk with 1.25mm (18 gauge) black wire. Thread it through the top of each block and wrap it around the nail, then do the same at the bottom until all three pieces are firm. Arrange moss and pebbles around the base of the trunk.

3 Make the basic topiary shape with foliage, leaving plenty of room for the flowers. Do not make the shape perfectly symmetrical or it will not look interesting. Here, eucalyptus was used to create the outline, and laurustinus to give depth and interest.

4 Use the large flowers to lend depth and the smaller ones to fill out the shape, but don't let them overcrowd each other. Here, I used 'Lovely Girl' roses and daisies. Fill in any gaps with foliage because it is not as obtrusive as flowers. If you are using only one type of flower, such as roses, place them in the ball first and add the foliage last to lighten and soften the overall shape. Keep spraying the topiary as the oasis will dry out very quickly. This arrangement may only last for one or two days.

MAKING A CONICAL DESIGN

1 To give this design balance, both visually and literally, you should use a heavy vase with a pedestal base. Build up a pyramid shape with blocks of wet oasis, but do not make the pyramid too high as the taller it is, the more unstable it becomes.

2 Trim the corners of the oasis with a knife to give a smoother base on which to work. Tightly cover the pyramid with wire netting, then secure it to the vase handles with black reel wire. Push green garden sticks deep into the oasis blocks to anchor them together, then trim the ends flush with the netting.

3 Push 1.25mm (18 gauge) stub wire through all the fruit and vegetables. Here, I used small pineapples, fennel hearts, apples, halved melons, grapes, plums and star fruit. Wire the fruits from different angles to create the maximum interest. For such heavy items as pineapples, you should use green garden sticks instead of wires.

4 When assembling the design it is best to start with the biggest pieces as they will form the basic shape. I fixed the pineapples, grapes and then the melons in place, before filling in with the smaller fruits. It is not necessary to use a great many flowers and foliage when working with this amount of fruit and vegetables (see pp 74–5 for the finished arrangement).

MAKING AN ALL-ROUND ARRANGEMENT

1 Place a quarter block of wet oasis into a china tazza vase, securing it with white oasis tape. Decide how high and wide you want the arrangement to be, then make the basic shape with one type of foliage — I used weigela. Place one piece slightly off-centre, about five pieces around the bottom edge so that the stems are flush with the bowl but coming from the focal point and three pieces in the middle.

2 Add the honeysuckle, again placing one piece slightly off-centre, then arrange some honeysuckle between the lowest pieces of weigela so that it trails over the bowl and softens any hard lines. Add more honeysuckle to the centre of the arrangement, making sure that it does not form a triangular shape but that the top pieces are the same length as those at the sides.

3 Add the phlox, using exactly the same principles as above, and always looking for space and filling it rather than crowding your original outlining materials.

4 Starting at the top, add the scabious, then add the bottom pieces and finally the middle ones. You should not end up with a point in the middle or at the sides, and the foliage should flow gently out from the sides of the bowl.

MAKING A
MANTELPIECE ARRANGEMENT

This is assembled in a long trough-shaped vase that fits the width of the mantelpiece. I used blossom, lilac, lilies, 'Evelyn' spray roses, hydrangeas, eucalyptus, ivy and silver pear foliage.

The most important point to remember when creating an arrangement on a ledge of any sort is to keep the balance correct. For example, you should ensure that you don't have a lot of heavy flowers that jut too far out of the front of the arrangement, as this could overbalance the whole container. To prevent this happening, place such items as the lilac towards the back of the arrangement and cut the ones to be used at the front quite short and close to the vase.

In fact, if you were to look at the side of this arrangement, you would see that the flowers do not extend more than 12.5–15cm (5–6in) over the ledge. Trailing ivy placed along the top of the mantelpiece and down over the front helps to link the arrangement with its surroundings and to soften the lines of the mantelpiece itself.

I used cream lilies rather than white, which are probably a more usual choice, because the lilac and roses have a similar strength of colour and therefore white would have been too sharp and stark a contrast. The hydrangeas were chosen to give the arrangement depth and add tones of soft pink and lime green.

DECORATING A CANDELABRA

Decorating a candelabra is a charming idea and is made easy with the use of candle cups. Oasis cylinders can then be fitted into the candle cups to hold the flowers and foliage in place. Decorated candelabras are ideal for dinner parties as they can either be placed on a sideboard or used as the table centrepiece.

To decorate a candelabra, place the oasis cylinder in the candle cup, put the candle holder in the middle, then tape the oasis into the dish and add the candle. Place all of this in the candelabra, then add the foliage first and finally the flowers. I used 'Champagne' roses, berried eucalyptus, tea roses, ivy, euphorbia and mixed garden foliage. When decorating the candelabra,

you must ensure that the arrangement cascades down over the candle cup to hide it, and drapes over the candlesticks. You can also make a smaller arrangement in a candle cup for a single candlestick.

The central point of the arrangement will be approximately 2.5cm (1in) above the dish, and all the flowers and foliage should be arranged in such a way that the stems are angled towards this one point. For example, the rose on the bottom right-hand side was put into the arrangement from the same angle at which it finally lay. This principle should be remembered when working with any arrangement, as you will then find that your flowers look more natural when arranged.

Over page, left *The trailing foliage in this arrangement helps to link it with its surroundings.* Over page, right *Flowers give this candelabra the perfect finishing touch.*

Celebrating with Flowers

Every special occasion deserves to be celebrated with flowers, whether it is a relaxing weekend breakfast or a stylish, once-in-a-lifetime wedding. This section of the book has been divided into different occasions, full of ideas, advice and photographs to help you turn any event into a unique celebration with the help of flowers.

WEDDINGS

Of all special and celebratory occasions, weddings must be one of the most glorious. In fact, it is hard to imagine a wedding without flowers for they help to set the scene, and their beauty, colour and possible fragrance all contribute towards ensuring that the day is a joyful and memorable one.

My advice for any bride wanting to plan her wedding flowers is first to decide on the effect she wishes to create. The style of a wedding can vary considerably, with frills and fantasy, unusual and original, or strictly traditional being just three of the many options. Other important considerations include money, the season, the wedding venue, whether it takes place in a town or the country, and the colour theme of the wedding. I find that many brides prefer to allocate most of their budget to the flowers, since they can turn even the most uninspiring reception area into a spectacular setting, and the exuberance of their colour and form echoes perfectly the happiness of the occasion.

If you use a florist at your wedding, rather than decide to arrange the flowers yourself, you should ask them to visit the venue with you in advance, as they may well have some decorating ideas that had not occurred to you, or be able to suggest ways of camouflaging or drawing attention away from any unsightly areas.

As the wedding dress is usually considered to be one of the most important factors, its design and colour will take precedence over the bridal bouquet and flowers. The style of your dress will also dictate your hairstyle, and therefore determine the flowers for the head dress. If you are unsure of which flowers to choose, do ask the florist for advice.

You may find it useful to make a list of your favourite flowers first, as well as any that you dislike, and if the florist has a shop you should visit it to have a good look at the stock. Discuss the list with them, as they will be able to tell you whether or not a particular flower will be available at the time

of your wedding. I would also suggest that you return to the florist's shop two weeks before your wedding in case any flowers are being sold that you have not thought of, yet may prefer.

Unfortunately, some flowers, no matter how beautiful, are simply not suitable for bouquets or head dresses because they don't last long out of water, and certainly not throughout the day: peonies, sweet peas, lilac and anemones all come into this category. There is nothing worse than seeing a bride, coming out of church or halfway through the speeches, who is carrying or wearing a sad collection of drooping, wilting, flowers. If you've set your heart on using any of these flowers they will have to be incorporated into a table or pedestal arrangement instead. Amongst the many flowers and foliage that can be used in bouquets and head dresses with great success are roses, stephanotis, lily of the valley (if wired), rue, ivy, jasmine, ranunculus, tuberoses, chincherinchees, bridal gladioli, lilies and carnation petals.

If you will be having attendants, their colouring will play a large part in the choice of their outfits and of their flowers. For instance, you should avoid peaches and strong pinks for anyone who is redheaded, but most pastel colours will blend in well and look pretty. It is very attractive for all the flowers of the bridal party to co-ordinate, but that may not always be possible. Instead, you could ensure that one colour forms the theme that links you with your matron of honour, bridesmaids, pages, flower girl or ring bearer.

If you are to be married in a church or synagogue, there may be several architectural features that will lend themselves to floral decoration. Naturally,

Facing page To gain maximum impact from your arrangements in a church, incorporate existing features in your designs. Over page The glorious colours of the stained glass window were a major factor in the choice of flowers for this wedding.

you should first consult the priest or rabbi, just to check that they have no objections, and in fact they may want to discuss the flowers with you anyway. Do take note of everything that they say, particularly if they mention any restrictions, and abide by what they tell you – it may be your day, but it is their place of worship. This rule applies whether it is you or a florist who does the decorations.

It is important when arranging flowers, whatever the venue, to use the areas that lend themselves to the flowers rather than creating free-standing arrangements that are then dotted about seemingly willy-nilly. This will ensure that the decorations look much more natural and are in keeping with their environment.

If the organ is old, you might be able to

The pale pinks and greens of these pew ends are perfectly suited to their dark wood backgrounds. Facing page *Incorporated into a pillar plaque, the varied colours and forms of these flowers and foliage are easily visible above the heads of the congregation.*

decorate part of it (*see p 40*). Here, I arranged artichoke leaves, red euphorbia, cream larkspur, trichilium and sweet peas on a long oasis tray using one block of wet oasis wrapped in wire netting. It is also essential to anchor the back of the arrangement in place with plenty of wire, which will stop it toppling forward once the flowers have been arranged.

I had to wire the bottoms of the artichoke leaves before inserting them in the oasis, as their stems would have disintegrated

otherwise. The red euphorbia was used to bring some colour forward from the background of the crest. This arrangement is also suitable for decorating window sills, as you will be able to use the same oasis tray and basic shape.

Arrangements on pew ends are a marvellous way of decorating aisles, because not only do they look beautiful but also, if you have chosen your flowers carefully, they will release their fragrance as the guests walk past. In fact, I think it is almost essential to decorate wide aisles and dark wood, otherwise the church or synagogue can look bare and not festive enough for such a special occasion. When planning pew end decorations it is important to consider not only the shape of the pews themselves but also the width of the aisle.

This will dictate your floral design, because if the aisle is very narrow, the bridal procession, as well as the guests, may brush against the flowers and inadvertently spoil them. Here, however, the aisle was so wide that I was able to make large arrangements that protruded quite a way into the aisle, with no fear of them being damaged.

It is always best to assemble the arrangements *in situ*, at least until you learn the exact shape and method with which to create them. Otherwise, if you make them

You may be asked to keep the altar arrangements small, but they should still be visually strong and well defined. Facing page *Use flowers to draw attention to any existing features, such as this carved stonework.*

on a floor, you will find that large gaps are visible between the oasis and the pews when they are hung in position, thereby revealing all your mechanics. If you do have to make them up beforehand, try to work with them hanging from something that is roughly of the same width and height as the pews for which they are intended.

To make these 'pew ends' as florists call them, I used quarter blocks of wet oasis, wrapped in wire netting and then backed with plastic sheeting (*see pp 20–1*). Before the flowers were arranged in place, I attached the pew ends to their pews with loops of silver wire, very firmly secured to the wire netting. The wires were then concealed with pale pink ribbon. It is very important to ensure that the wires are firm, and strong enough to take the damp oasis. You don't want the pew ends to crash to the floor in the middle of the service! You can buy oasis pew ends that are already made up, ready for the addition of the flowers, but I still prefer to do all the mechanics myself as I will then definitely know that they are secure. To decorate these pew ends I used 'Evelyn' spray roses, cream, white and pink sweet peas, eucalyptus, euphorbia and Doris pinks.

If there aren't any pews in the building in which you will be married, you could instead place oasis trays, filled with flowers, by the sides of the chairs ranged down the aisle. Of course, you will have to ensure that it will be easy for the guests to get in and out of the rows of chairs without treading or slipping on the flowers.

Arrangements on pillars or walls are also an excellent idea, either for a small church or for a large wedding, as they will be easily seen whether the guests are standing up or sitting down. I made a pillar plaque with pink peonies, rubrum lilies, *Alchemilla*

The pretty colours and intriguing shape of this archway not only make it an attractive frame for the statue in the background but also mean it is ideal as a setting for photographs of the wedding party.

mollis, burgundy stock and eucalyptus. The burgundy is quite an unusual colour to use for a wedding, as you will probably have noticed that most brides tend to choose pink and white, peach and cream or yellow and white flowers. However, I feel that using a darker colour gives a rich, lush look to the whole arrangement, and using flowers with a strong scent helps to cover what may well be the church's own rather musty smell.

To secure the plaque to the pillar you will have to find an existing nail or hook on which to hang it. Even if the only nail is on the opposite side of the pillar, you will be able to attach a length of wire through the wire netting that has been wrapped around the wet oasis (*see pp 20–1*) and secure it in the right position. Alternatively, you may have to suspend the plaque from the top of the pillar. These arrangements should be made a good five or six hours before the wedding, by which time they should have stopped dripping water.

Before planning an arrangement for the altar you will have to check that it will be permitted. In some cases a small arrangement that is not too obtrusive is acceptable, although anything larger would not be. At Veevers Carter Flowers, if we are able to decorate the altar, and its background is not particularly interesting, we sometimes use Italian lily vases filled with white lilies and perhaps some eucalyptus. Always try to keep any altar decorations very clean and sharp, as they have to be seen from a distance and if you use dark or coloured flowers they tend to disappear against the ornate nature of the altar cloths. Here, we filled glass *tazzas* with hosta leaves, red euphorbia and large white lilies, holding them in place with wire netting. Any oasis would have been visible and also made it difficult for the flowers and foliage to absorb enough water. The red euphorbia was used to accentuate the red tones in the background painting.

Large arrangements or pedestals are another way of decorating a church, and are often placed by the steps leading up to the altar or by the altar itself, depending on the size of the building. As you will notice in the main photograph of the church (*see pp 42–3*), the flowers in the pedestal arrangements were specially chosen to bring forward the colours of the stained glass windows. This is not always common practice at weddings, since the bride normally likes all the flowers to echo precisely her colour theme, but in this case the windows of the church dominated her choice. As the bride's colours were pink and white, we used white, pink and lime green in the pew ends and chose lime green and white to connect them with the pedestal arrangements.

An ideal example of the effectiveness of letting the surroundings dictate the floral decoration is to create an archway (*see p 29*). Here, we built one in a large garden, but it would look equally attractive if arranged in a church. I don't think it is important for an archway to be symmetrical when it is outdoors, but if you were to create it in a church you should follow the existing lines of the architecture. For this garden, I used Doris pinks, white campanulas, wild gypsophila, lavender sweet peas and *Alchemilla mollis*.

An archway makes a most attractive frame for a bride and groom, especially when the wedding photographs are taken, and provides a very pretty focal point for any garden or walkway. If the garden in which the reception will be held already has a pergola or arch over which flowering plants have been trained, you might

Below *A foot corsage made from a few small flowers is a delightful accessory for both bride and bridesmaids.* Facing page *A mixed bouquet is a striking departure from wedding tradition.*

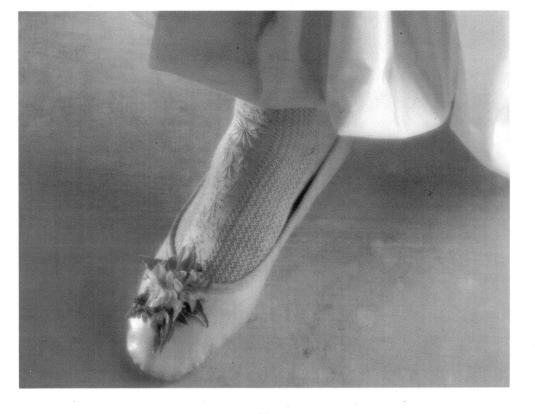

consider taking advantage of it and holding your wedding when the flowers will be in full bloom. If they aren't, you can always help nature along with a few strategically placed blocks of flowers that you have arranged yourself. However, you must make sure that the flowers are well clear of people's heads and that any thorny stems have been removed to avoid accidents.

Whether you are planning the flowers for a bride or a bridesmaid, you must always bear in mind the colours of the background against which the flowers will be seen, such as the dress. For example, if the colour scheme for the wedding flowers is pale pink and white, the flowers will work perfectly against a pale background, but if the background is darker you will have to bring the colour through using flowers that are a slightly darker pink. When choosing the flowers for a very strongly-coloured dress, such as the one shown in the photograph on the facing page, any pale, insipid flowers would have stood out too much and looked quite wrong. Instead, the colours used in the posy and head dress strike a perfect balance with the dress.

For the posy, I used champagne roses, 'Blushing Bride' proteas and delphinium heads, with more delphiniums and proteas for the head dress. Most of the time I prefer to use foliage in my arrangements but it would have been unnecessary here and in fact would have detracted from the luscious feeling of the posy and head dress.

For the bride who wants to make a dramatic entrance, a colourful mixed bouquet is the perfect choice. White, or cream, flowers may still be the shades to choose for traditional weddings but tastes are changing, and coloured flowers can offer much more scope for anyone wanting to show their individuality. An enormous wealth of different shades, shapes, textures and scents is available from florists now, making it much easier for a bride to choose a bouquet that suits her personality, matches her dress or is the focus for her overall colour scheme, therefore bringing a

sense of continuity, rhythm and harmony to the day through the flowers she chooses.

Here, the bouquet was composed of white tulips, muscari, jasmine, lily of the valley, cyclamen leaves, pink ranunculus, variegated ivy and laurustinus. The heady scents of the jasmine and lily of the valley blend together well, in addition to lending extra romance to the bouquet. As the bride walks up the aisle and all heads turn in her direction, the perfume from her bouquet will linger in the air for added impact. To avoid her own scent clashing with that of the bouquet, she should wear none at all, choose the essential oil from a particular flower (both jasmine and lily of the valley are easily available), or wear a perfume that contains one or more of the flowers in its base notes.

The bouquet itself is pear-shaped, with the wired flowers loosely arranged to give them some natural movement. The lighter flowers around the edges were planned to break up any hard lines from the green foliage and further accentuate the soft feeling of the bouquet. A contrasting shape and texture was given to the centre of the arrangement by the small cyclamen leaves, with the delicate ivy and jasmine trails used to soften the tail of the bouquet.

To continue the theme of the bouquet, the head dress was made from baby tea roses, pink hyacinths, muscari, small 'Carte Blanche' roses, snowdrops, laurustinus, baby cyclamen leaves and single variegated ivy leaves. They were wired on to a circlet (*see pp 16–17*) and finished with a cream satin ribbon tied in a bow at the back. The colours used in the head dress were lighter than those of the bouquet, to complement

Previous page, left *Scattering flowers through the hair gives an informal and pretty effect.* Previous page, right *The exotic forms of these flowers are perfectly complemented by the shape of the bouquet.* Facing page *The strong colours of this bridesmaid's dress must be matched by equally strongly-coloured flowers.*

the skin tones and hair colour of the bride.

The advantage of using such a wide range of flowers is that the bridesmaids could carry small posies composed of a selection of the flowers worn by the bride. This is particularly effective when the style and colour of the bridesmaids' dresses are complementary but different from that of the bride, as the flowers will form the linking theme between them. The bride's mother could also choose her corsage from the bride's flowers, selecting suitable shades to match her outfit.

A special finishing touch for a bridesmaid are tiny corsages stitched on to her shoes (see p 50). Here, hyacinth bells, muscari, snowdrops, variegated ivy and baby pink tea roses were wired on to the base of a clip-on bow and then sewn on the ballet pump (see p 26). It is important to keep an arrangement like this small and delicate, as it could easily look clumsy or ungainly if large flower heads were used. Tiny foot corsages like this are ideal accessories for ballerina-length or shorter dresses, where they can be seen to their full advantage. They can, of course, be worn by the bride as well as her bridesmaids.

Threading flowers through the hair is one of the prettiest bridal decorations, and is especially suitable for informal, country weddings. I made a circlet from white muscari, gypsophila, stephanotis, coral spray roses, pearl carnations and variegated ivy leaves, then wired up individual flowers with silver wires and gently pushed them through the bridesmaid's hair. Unfortunately the flowers will not stay in place when threaded through thin straight hair, but they will do so in curly hair or in hair that has been put up. This is a lovely finishing touch for a circlet worn by a bridesmaid, or can be worn by the bride instead of a veil.

As an alternative to the bouquet shown on page 51, which uses a smaller selection of flowers, the bride's bouquet pictured on page 53 is dramatically full and luscious, with the large pale pink lilies acting as the focal point. I also used roses, freesias, chincherinchees, ivy and eucalyptus. If you wish, when wiring up the bouquet (see pp 14–15) you can remove the stamens from the lilies, as the yellow pollen they carry can easily stain fabrics or skin. The very pale yellow of the roses offsets and enhances the delicate pinks of the lilies and roses, giving the bouquet an overall soft pastel colouring.

Of all the many different locations suitable for a wedding reception, a marquee can be one of the most stunning and impressive. In addition, it can be one of the most convenient, providing you have a garden large enough to accommodate it, since not only will you not be so reliant on fine weather but also you will be able to hold the reception at home without having to rearrange your actual house. Marquees are available in a variety of sizes, styles and prices, with awnings and without, and ranging from the modest to the frankly luxurious, but even so most of them benefit from some floral decorations.

If you will be using a marquee with a special entrance, you can give it extra impact and style by flanking that entrance with stone urns filled with a riot of flowers. They will help to create a party-like atmosphere in the guests even before they enter the marquee, and if there is to be a receiving line the guests will have something to look at and talk about while they are waiting to greet the bridal party.

In this arrangement I used forsythia, white delphiniums, blue bee, pink and yellow antirrhinums, alstroemeria and blossom, which were arranged in a large bowl filled with wire netting. This was then placed in the stone urn. The mixed colourings in this arrangement are not only suitable for weddings but also birthdays, garden parties or any other occasions that

Facing page The impact of a flower-filled stone urn makes a magnificent first impression for wedding guests. Over page A wooden trellis can turn the inside of a marquee into a bower of flowers.

call for the use of a marquee.

It is particularly lovely to decorate a marquee with strongly-scented flowers, as they will fill the air with their perfume, just as flowers would if you were walking through a garden. It is always important that floral arrangements should look as natural as possible, and I feel that this is even more important when they are intended for a marquee, because of the outdoor ambience that will already exist.

Because of the quantity of flowers normally used when decorating a marquee, it is best to make up the arrangements the day before, ensuring that all the oasis is kept wet and the flowers sprayed as often as possible to keep them fresh. This is not such a problem in the winter, because of the lower temperatures, but even so you will have to ensure that the heaters that are normally used to warm up the marquee are not turned on until an hour before the guests arrive, or at least as late as possible to avoid the flowers wilting prematurely.

Decorating the interior of a marquee is largely a matter of choice, and will also be determined by the colours of the sides and ceiling. As with any other large space, a few large arrangements will create more impact than several smaller ones, the effect of which may be lost once all the guests are assembled. However, one area that benefits from being decorated is that around the wedding cake. I placed posies of flowers and trails of ivy on the trellis panels behind the wedding cake, to give a very pretty backdrop for the bride and groom when cutting the cake. I find that placing two pedestals on the floor at either side of the cake table is not only slightly dangerous but can also detract attention from the bride. In addition, they use up what may be very valuable floor space, especially when all the guests gather around the cake table during the speeches and toasts.

To make the posies, you should wrap quarter blocks of oasis in wire netting, then wire them on to the trellis work and decorate them *in situ* (*see p 19*). I used chincherinchees, maidenhair fern, cream spray carnations, ranunculus and 'Lovely Girl' roses, although of course you should choose the flowers that blend with or match those worn by the bride. The trails of ivy can be threaded through the trellis work to give a natural effect.

The silk swags around the cake table itself were held in place by posies that matched the decoration on top of the cake (*see pp 22–3*). Swags of material are sometimes preferable to trails of ivy or smilax, especially when they are finished off with little posies and bows. As a final touch, you can sprinkle flowers and petals across the tablecloth to accentuate the cake.

Garlands of flowers looped around the poles that support the marquee can look extremely pretty (*see pp 20–1*), and can also give you plenty of scope for departing from tradition and letting your individuality and style shine through. For example, in the photograph on the facing page I ignored the usual pink and white, yellow and white or peach and cream colours that are seen at so many weddings, and instead chose a particularly striking combination of colours to give the impression of lushness and abundance. A very great part of the charm of these garlanded poles is the ragged texture and shape of the parrot tulips, which echo the frothy outlines of the maidenhair fern. Variegated pittosporum ties in the yellow of the roses with the green of the other foliage.

If you are providing occasional tables for your guests, the marquee will look very attractive if you can decorate each one with a small arrangement of flowers. Here, I filled a small glass fish bowl with 'Lovely Girl' roses, blue bee, yellow ranunculus, chincherinchees, large pink lilies and maidenhair fern for a light, informal arrangement. If the day of the wedding is sunny, the light will reflect through the glass and water.

The bold colours of these garlands make them perfect for a summer wedding.

CHRISTENINGS

When planning a christening, tradition insists that it is blue for a boy and pink for a girl, but there are no rules saying when yellow and white, peach and cream or any other soft pastel colours should be used. In fact, using different colours can come as a welcome and refreshing change, and often prove to be the best option when several babies are being christened at one time.

When choosing flowers for a christening, I think it is important to use small delicate flowers rather than large and dramatic ones. After all, the flowers are really to welcome the baby into the world, and to emphasise the fact that babies themselves are tiny and fragile. As a useful rule to remember whenever you choose flowers, try to make them part of the occasion itself, rather than floral decorations that have been seemingly chosen at random. Successful flower arrangements should be natural and flowing, looking as though they have taken no time or trouble to arrange, even if the truth belies that fact, and this is especially appropriate when planning the flowers for a christening.

Although christening cakes only consist of one tier, and are often fairly plainly iced, decorating them with a few flowers can create a very pretty and attractive impression. If both the cake and the tablecloth are white or cream, arranging a light garland of foliage around the bottom of the cake will give it distinction and set it apart from its surroundings. You can also arrange a ring of flowers around the top edge of the cake, but do make sure you choose flowers and foliage that are not poisonous – for this reason you should avoid any flowers grown from bulbs, for example.

Whatever style of floral arrangement used for a christening, you must ensure that any flowers that will be near the baby do not have any thorns or pollen, nor a very strong scent, as these can easily irritate very small children. You must also check that you do not use anything that might be poisonous or a danger to children if they touch it.

When planning the decorations for a party following a christening, as well as the more usual arrangements, one charming idea is to decorate a crib (*see pp 64–5*). It makes a very pretty decoration for the corner of a room, or when placed beside the christening cake. Here, I used a mixture of jasmine, anemones, lily of the valley, white azaleas, de-thorned tea roses, wax flower and smilax for garlanding.

To make the flower garland for the top of the crib, cut a block of wet oasis into eight pieces, then wrap each one in wire netting (*see p 19*) and secure to the top edge of the crib with wire, ensuring that any sharp ends are facing outwards rather than inwards, and do not present a danger to the baby. If you are intending actually to place the baby in the cot, it might be a good idea to tie the oasis blocks in place with string or ribbon for safety's sake. Even though the flowers here are not poisonous, the baby should only be placed in the cot for photographs or short periods of supervised time, in case the baby tries to eat any of the petals or leaves. Garlands of smilax are arranged around the bottom edge of the crib, and finished off here with double bows of yellow satin ribbon.

I think that one of the prettiest ways of celebrating a baptism or christening is to decorate the font itself. Of course, it does help if the font is very old or made from carved stone, but even the most angular and modern font can be decorated with a few flowers. As with all other floral decorations that you have planned for a place of worship, you must discuss your ideas with the priest or minister first, and ask their permission before going ahead with your designs. If several babies will be baptised at the same time you should, of

Facing page If you wish to decorate a christening cake with fresh flowers and foliage, you should keep the icing as plain as possible for maximum effect. Over page Small delicate flowers are the best choice for christenings.

course, confer with the other parents who will be attending the ceremony to ascertain their choice of colour and flowers. They may be happy to let you arrange the flowers but, if that is not the case, you could make up your arrangement on the font and then carefully transfer it to a large board, ensuring that the pieces are kept in the right order, replacing them on the font when your baby is due to be baptised.

To create this arrangement, you should cut a block of wet oasis into four lengthways, cover one side of each piece in plastic and then evenly space them on top of the font, plastic side down, leaving a gap of at least 30cm (12in) where the priest will stand. Here, I used lavender sweet peas, 'Little Silver' and baby pink roses from which the thorns had been removed, cow parsley and eucalyptus, although you could use ivy instead. First, the cow parsley was arranged to make the overall shape, ensuring that it did not become too wide or trail into the bowl of the font. Then I added the sweet peas, roses and eucalyptus. It is important to make the arrangement on the font itself as this will help you to achieve the right shape and height. It will also enable you to check that you have covered all the oasis and plastic with either foliage or flowers. If well sprayed and kept in a cool place, this arrangement should last for about two days.

A simple bunch of lilies of the valley is an ideal present for the mother of the child, sent on the morning of the christening. Facing page *When decorating the font, be sure to leave a space for the priest or minister to conduct the service.*

ANNIVERSARIES

Giving flowers is a marvellous way of saying congratulations, 'I love you' or any other special message, and they help to create a romantic atmosphere whether you are part of the celebration yourself or simply a well-wisher. In this chapter you will find just some of the different shapes and colour schemes you can use for anniversary flowers, but there are no hard and fast rules.

Thinking about the meaning of each anniversary may give you plenty of ideas. For example, you could arrange some pot-pourri in a papier mâché bowl (paper – first anniversary); make a planted basket and swathe it in a beautiful material (cotton – second); put an arrangement in a leather-covered vase or the pen-holder of a leather desk set (leather – third); create a table decoration from fruit and flowers (fruit and flowers – fourth); fill a wooden pot with interesting fruits and foliage (wood – fifth); make a bowl from crystallized sugar, containing an arrangement of dried or artificial flowers (sugar – sixth); make a needlepoint or crewel work picture of the original wedding bouquet (wool – seventh); fill a bronze or copper pot with flowers (bronze – eighth); arrange some long flowing grasses in a tall pottery urn (pottery – ninth); fill an item of thirties' chrome with gardenia plants (tin – tenth); arrange a breakfast tray with lovely linen and a small floral decoration (silk and fine linen – twelfth); fill a crystal vase with flowers (crystal – fifteenth); fill a porcelain vase with flowers (china – twentieth); line the bottom of a glass fish bowl with pearls, then fill it with marine-like plants and flowers (pearl – thirtieth); create an arrangement of coral-coloured flowers (coral – thirty-fifth); fill a dark green vase with an arrangement of mixed foliage (fifty-fifth – emerald); arrange a mixture of blue bee and delphiniums in a tall vase (sapphire – sixty-fifth); attach a piece of platinum jewellery to a flower arranged in a frosted glass lily vase (platinum – seventieth).

For the ruby anniversary arrangement, shown on the facing page, I chose a predominantly red and pink theme, with red 'Moss Roses', 'Only One' and 'Carol' roses. Green guelder roses were chosen as a contrast to the reds and pinks, with the grey of the eucalyptus and pussy willow accentuating the warm tones of the roses. The flowers and foliage were arranged in an all-round design, in wire netting and water so that the flowers would keep fresh for as long as possible. In this arrangement, notice how the flowers break the edges of the vase, softening the lines. When using roses, you must ensure that either flowers or foliage break up the main outline of the arrangement, to avoid there being just a solid lump of roses. Here, the eucalyptus and pussy willow are used to great effect. With the host of red and pink flowers available, you can create many different arrangements to celebrate a ruby wedding, perhaps choosing the favourite flowers of one of the recipients, or some of the flowers used in the original bouquet.

When creating an arrangement to celebrate a silver wedding anniversary, you could be guided by the cool elegance of the metal itself. For my arrangement (*see pp 70–1*), I created a very romantic atmosphere through my choice of flowers and foliage. I used cow parsley, 'Little Silver' roses, white stock, moluccella, eucalyptus and pittosporum, arranged in wire netting to keep the cow parsley and roses at their best. The *tazza* shape of the glass bowl and the delicious scent of the stocks added to the overall impact of the arrangement, with its mixture of pointed, round and frothy shapes.

You might consider using artificial flowers: their standard, quality and availability are improving all the time, with the result that they are now far more

Facing page *The different shapes and colours of the roses in this arrangement add interest and variety.* Over page *As well as giving out a magnificent scent, the texture and form of the white stocks echoes that of the moluccella.*

realistic and attractive than ever before.

To create this arrangement for a diamond wedding anniversary, I chose silk roses of varying shapes and colours, cream alstroemeria, slightly waxed artificial maple leaves and dusted artificial plums. I set them in brown oasis, placed in a white china bowl, in a facing arrangement. You can buy roses and alstroemeria at almost any time of year, so there is no need to worry about displaying the arrangement when the flowers are out of season.

The flowers used here are all hand-wrapped, which makes it impossible to stand them with fresh flowers in water, but there is an enormous range of plastic-stemmed flowers that can be used in this way and which are just as pretty. Artificial flowers can be used with dried flowers, perhaps when you want a colour that is not available in dried form.

The best way to care for artificial flowers is to blow any dust off them gently with a hairdryer, although polyester flowers can be washed by hand. Using a small amount of washing-up liquid and warm water, plunge them in and out of the water, but don't rub them as they may fray. Shake them to remove excess moisture, then hang them upside down over a waterproof surface until dry (a bath or basin is ideal). Keep them out of sunlight and away from radiators or other sources of strong heat.

You do not always have to use a predominance of flowers in an arrangement, as the golden wedding anniversary pyramid (*see pp 74–5*) illustrates so effectively. Using fruit has created a design that is very unusual and full of surprises – the more one looks at it, the more one can see another element or different shape. I chose fennel, apples, grapes, baby pineapples, melons, golden plums and star fruits, with 'Golden Shower' orchids, parrot tulips, amaryllis, tuberoses and eucalyptus.

The pyramid is constructed on a mound of oasis, placed in a heavy lead vase for maximum stability, and then covered with wire netting (*see p 33*). You will notice that the flowers don't overcrowd the fruit, so that all the shapes are visible, and you should use the flowers to accentuate the fruit rather than hide it. If you keep spraying it with water the arrangement should last for about five days. However, don't be tempted to eat the fruit as most of it will have been pinned in place with wires and will therefore be inedible.

This type of arrangement has to be constructed *in situ*, as the enormous weight of the finished article makes it very difficult and cumbersome to transport, and you could even dislodge parts of it in the process. You must also work on a very sturdy surface to avoid the pyramid toppling over. This type of arrangement is marvellous for a table centrepiece or decoration for a buffet table.

Facing page *Just like diamonds, this diamond wedding anniversary arrangement should last forever – it is made from artificial flowers!* Over page *The rich colours of the lush flowers and unusual fruits make this pyramid truly exotic.*

ROMANTIC OCCASIONS

No romance is complete without flowers – their lovely colours, shapes and scents add an extra dimension to special occasions and can provide wonderful memories.

Traditionally, flowers have always been given meanings, a practice that grew during Victorian times when seemingly almost every plant had a particular significance. Even today, many brides like to choose their wedding flowers for their romantic meanings, and can be very surprised and dismayed on discovering that their favourite flowers represent something rather negative or sad.

However, there is no need to confine this charming tradition to purely weddings, and you can create anything from a table decoration to a posy that bears a floral message. On the facing page, I have arranged just a few of the very many flowers that have particular meanings. Reading clockwise, they are:

Burgundy rose – unconscious beauty

Lily of the valley – return of happiness

Blue garden anemone – forsaken

Rosemary – remembrance

Ivy – fidelity, marriage

Jonquil – I desire a return of affection

Amaryllis – pride, splendid beauty

Sweet william – gallantry

Purple lilac – first emotions of love

Daisy – innocence

Orchid – rare beauty

Primrose – early youth

Hyacinth – sport, play

Pink carnation – woman's love

Fern – sincerity

Food often plays an important part in romantic occasions, and one marvellous way to celebrate a special meal with a loved one is to create a stunning table decoration.

If it is to be placed in the centre of the table, you will have to make an all-round arrangement, ensuring that it is not tall enough to obscure the diners' views of each other – no one wants to have to peer through a forest of leaves and flowers!

In my arrangement, I chose the flowers and foliage for their prettiness and delicacy, which helped to emphasise the romance of the occasion. I used gypsophila to give softness, orchids for their exotic qualities, sprigs of rosemary for their interesting shapes, tendrils of variegated ivy for their colour contrast and shape, pink tulips and ranunculus for their different shapes and textures, muscari to give some contrast in colour, and lilies of the valley for their softness and delicious scent. Before creating the arrangement, I placed some wet oasis in a very low bowl which was completely hidden by the flowers once they were in position.

A very simple but effective addition to a romantic table is to choose an attractive cloth (unless, of course, you wish to admire a beautiful table top) and scatter petals and leaves across it. Here, I placed a 'Carol' rose by each plate and laid a few ivy leaves on the cloth to link it to the arrangement and give the table a relaxed air. You can also add other small touches.

The wearing of flowers also has romantic associations. Buttonholes and corsages are well-known, but a corsage is not always suitable as it can ruin the line of a dress. Many women prefer a wrist corsage. It makes a stunning change from a bracelet or wristwatch, and is an unexpected finishing touch to a short or three-quarter length

Facing page Some of the flowers that have been assigned special meanings. Over page Although flowers play a major role in the success of a romantically decorated table, beautiful china and linen are also important.

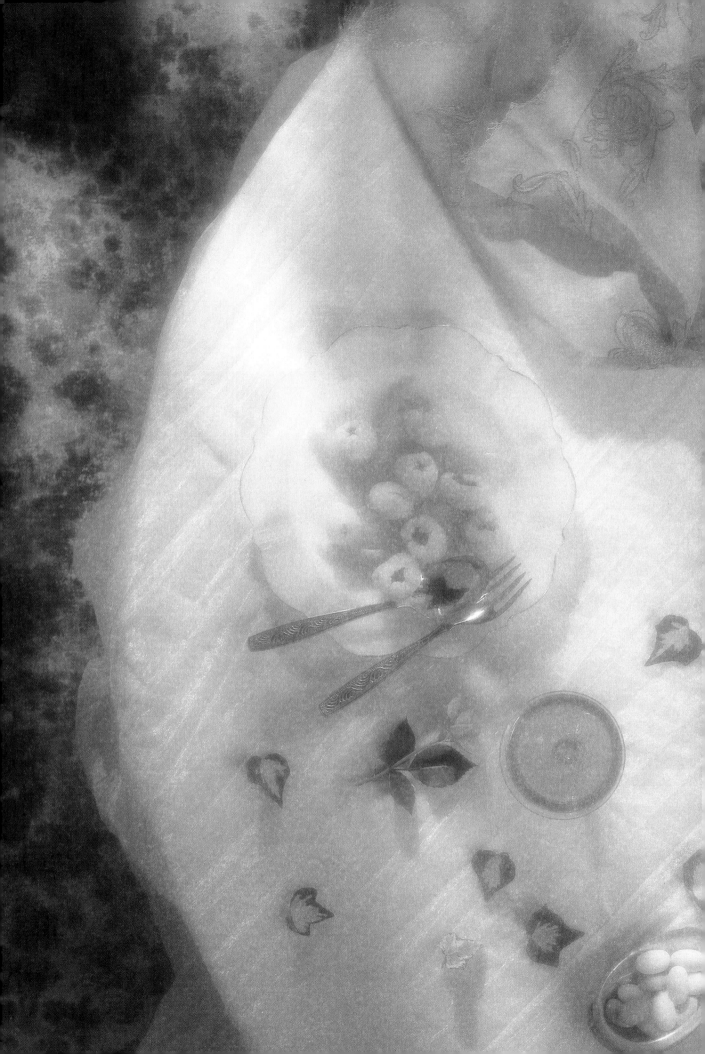

sleeve. You can also adapt the idea for a bride or bridesmaid.

When making a wrist corsage, it is best to choose small dainty flowers, as anything that is too large or cumbersome will look unbalanced or out of place. I like a colour theme of white and green because it is fresh and tones with almost any outfit. If there will be no contrast in the colour of the flowers, you should create a contrast in texture and shape instead – I used white freesias, white ranunculus and white euphorbia, with variegated ivy as foliage.

To make the corsage, first measure the circumference of the wrist by wrapping a length of satin ribbon around it, allowing extra at each end – this will be used when the corsage is tied around the wrist with a neat bow, hidden from sight. Then, wire each flower and piece of foliage individually, before covering with gutta percha. Wire the flowers and foliage on to the ribbon, as you would a head dress (*see pp 16–17*), then cover the wired part of the ribbon with gutta percha. The finished corsage should not be too heavy, and will last for about ten hours from the time it is made.

A tight Victorian posy makes a lovely accessory to a ballgown, and can be taken to a formal dinner or party. This type of posy is only successful if it is wired very tightly together, otherwise it will lose its shape. The benefit of this is that even if the flowers start to wilt, they will only be noticeable if you look very carefully.

Wire all the flowers individually with silver and stub wires, then cover them with gutta percha before assembling the posy tightly in your hand. Start with the centre of the posy and work outwards, arranging it so that, when viewed sideways, it is slightly raised in the middle and slopes downwards to the outer edges. The finishing touch is provided by an outer frill of lace or paper.

Working from the centre of the posy outwards, I used a single 'Carol' rose, then rows of violets, white freesias, 'Carol' roses, muscari, gypsophila, variegated ivy and rose leaves. This contrast of colour makes it easy to match the posy to most interiors or outfits, although it can of course be created in other colours or using varieties of just one flower, such as roses.

Above A floral wrist corsage is a charming accessory. Facing page The tighter the flowers are packed together in this posy, the more effective and long-lasting they will be.

FLOWERS FOR MOTHER'S DAY

What better way of spoiling your mother – or someone who is your mother in all but name – than to give her a pretty posy of flowers to celebrate Mother's Day? Very often the simplest arrangements are the most effective, as they can display the flowers in their true beauty, so don't worry if you can't reach a florist in time – a few flowers picked from the garden can be just as impressive and attractive as those bought from a shop, especially if the recipient prefers them.

For many busy mothers, the ultimate luxury is being brought breakfast in bed, especially if it is arranged on a pretty tray. Choosing a small bunch of flowers to match the china or an embroidered napkin is a particularly pretty decoration. The flowers used here are primroses, muscari and their leaves, arranged in a small glass vase, to keep the design very simple and fresh.

A large tied posy of feminine, scented flowers, held together with a length of white satin ribbon, is another idea for a Mother's Day present (*see p 84*), although it needs to be more carefully planned than a simple vase of flowers. Nevertheless, once again the flowers do not have to be bought from a florist, and a good hunt through the garden may produce a sizeable bunch of suitable flowers. If possible, when collecting the flowers, choose the ones that you know your mother likes, rather than your own personal favourites, unless, of course, the two coincide.

To make the tied posy illustrated here, I stripped off their lower leaves, then gathered the double pink tulips, paper-white narcissi, pink ranunculus and eucalyptus leaves together in my hand, tied them together with ribbon and finished them with a big bow. Then, all the stems were trimmed to the same length, so that the flowers could be placed in a container without any further arrangement. This always creates a very natural-looking posy that is suitable for most types of vase, and is especially appreciated by people who do not have the time or the expertise to arrange flowers themselves.

Many people love the beauty of cut flowers, but feel that their joy is all too fleeting, in which case giving them a bowl or basket filled with living plants is the perfect solution, especially if it contains flowering plants as well as those loved for their foliage alone. If you are intending to give a planted bowl to a busy mother on Mother's Day, you will help her immeasurably by choosing plants that are easy to care for. Another important consideration is to select plants that require roughly the same amounts of light and moisture, and which look good together. I filled a bowl with dracaena, jasmine, a white hydrangea and a white azalea, to provide a good contrast of white and green. This combination of colours always creates a strong impact and gives a very fresh feel.

When planting the bowl, always remember to leave a small trench around the rim where the soil meets the bowl, so that you can water the plants easily without having any spills. You should also choose a container that is watertight and deep enough to house the plants and soil, as well as sturdy enough to bear their weight. The hydrangea, azalea and jasmine can be left in the garden during the summer months and brought indoors again during the winter, but the dracaena would have to be replanted in a separate container as it would not be happy outside. As well as being an unusual gift for Mother's Day, a planted bowl also makes an ideal present for someone who is bedridden or in hospital, as they will be able to watch the plants grow and enjoy them coming into flower.

Facing page *Grand or lavish flowers look out of place on a breakfast tray, so keep your arrangement fresh and simple.* Over page, left *Because a tied posy is arranged in the hand before being bound with ribbon, it can be placed in water without any further arrangement being necessary.* Over page, right *A small planted bowl makes a delightful Mother's Day present.*

CELEBRATING BIRTHDAYS

Flowers make the perfect birthday present for many people, whether you arrange them in a container that is part of the gift, tie them in a posy or bouquet, or simply pack them in a box. No matter what time of year the birthday occurs you should be able to find some suitable flowers.

It is always difficult to find a present for a man, and flowers aren't often thought of. I think it is a misconception that men don't like receiving flowers, although you may have to make a special effort to choose flowers with masculine overtones or colours – pastel pinks and primrose yellows may not go down very well! However, whites, greens, bold yellows, blues, oranges, rusts and dark peach are all acceptable for men, as they tend to prefer stronger colours. Planted bowls (*see p 85*) and little planted gardens, or standard or specimen plants, also make excellent presents for men. On the whole I think that arrangements of flowers or collections of plants are better options than cut flowers for men as the recipient will not have to fiddle with scissors or remember to keep topping up the water in the vase.

When choosing a container in which you will arrange some birthday flowers, either find one that will be an ideal receptacle, or select a bowl or basket that can be used for other purposes afterwards. I found a silver bowl, and filled it with rosemary, eucalyptus, muscari, hyacinths and anemones to make a strong and dramatic arrangement. The greys of the eucalyptus and rosemary form an excellent contrast with the blues and purples of the flowers, and the hyacinths provided a very strong and delicious scent.

Most grandparents enjoy a sense of tradition, so what better way to celebrate a grandmother's birthday than with a big tea party held especially for her? The classic floral decoration for such an occasion must be a big vase of flowers on the tea table, containing a selection of garden flowers or perhaps something a little more unusual. I made an arrangement (*see pp 88–9*) with 'Only One' roses, rusty Singapore orchids, 'Cheer' narcissi, 'Bahama' roses and red euphorbia. The orchids make a good contrast with the roses and narcissi, with the euphorbia softening the contrast between the cream and the red of the roses. The butter colour of the 'Bahama' roses forms the link from the very creamy tones of the narcissi through to the deep red of the 'Only One' roses. If I had just used the narcissi and the red roses, the colour contrast would have been too harsh, and I chose the orchids because they are out of the ordinary, cannot be picked from a garden and therefore give the arrangement added dimension, interest and a very exotic feel.

When working with such soft-stemmed flowers as narcissi, it is best to arrange them in water and wire netting rather than oasis, which will damage the stems. Oasis is also visible, and therefore unsightly, when using glass bowls or vases.

Another successful birthday present is a mixed bouquet of flowers, although these are usually only sent out by florists. However, if you can buy the correct type of cellophane, you could easily make up a bouquet yourself at home, to give a very professional and lavish effect. To ensure that the flowers reach their destination looking as fresh as possible, you should prick small holes in the cellophane after wrapping, and only make up the bouquet at the last minute.

For my mixed bouquet I chose 'Evelyn' spray roses, double pink tulips, September flower, 'Porcelain' roses, eucalyptus, blossom and 'La Rêve' lilies. When making up the bouquet, you should remember that someone will have to put it into a vase, so try to choose flowers and foliage that have

Facing page *Choose strong dark colours when selecting flowers for a man.* Over page *The use of orchids gives an added dimension and interest to this traditional tea table arrangement.*

relatively the same length of stem but vary in shape, to provide visual interest.

When receiving a bouquet, you should always cut, split or bash all the stems as they will have been out of water for at least one hour, if not longer, and will be in need of a good long drink. If the flowers have wilted you should condition them first, then place them in deep water for an hour or two before arranging them. This will ensure that you derive the maximum enjoyment and life from the flowers.

Should you wish to create the same impression but have not been able to buy the right type of cellophane, then a low cardboard box covered in plain or patterned paper, and lined with crumpled tissue paper, is an excellent alternative. The flowers will stay fresher if placed in a box, as you can wrap damp tissue paper around the ends of their stems, and spray the flowers themselves with a light mist of water to give added moisture. If you will be transporting the flowers to their recipient yourself, the box will provide added protection as it will support the flowers and prevent them bruising. To protect open lilies or similar flowers, you should gently wrap each flower head in tissue paper to stop the petals breaking or being crushed. In my flower box I used single cream chrysanthemums, cream tulips, 'Album' chrysanthemums, white ranunculus, laurustinus and rosemary.

When sending someone cut flowers, it is always a good idea to include foliage as well as flowers, to enable them to create an arrangement without having to buy any extras. I also believe that foliage helps to accentuate the flowers and adds contrasting shapes, textures and colours that make all the difference to the finished arrangement.

As a general tip, whenever you are carrying flowers and foliage from one place to another, perhaps to create an arrangement *in situ*, you should always transport them in a large cardboard box, padded with crumpled tissue paper and lightly sprayed with water. This will give them as much protection as possible and ensure that they arrive in good condition.

*When giving someone a present of cut flowers for them to arrange themselves, you can either wrap them in cellophane (*facing page*) or pack them into a box (*above*).*

EASTER FLOWERS

Easter – the very word conjures up images of trees bursting into bud, carpets of spring flowers and the first signs that summer is on the way. Even if Easter has no religious significance for you, nevertheless you can still derive a great deal of enjoyment and satisfaction from celebrating the arrival of spring and the visible rebirth of life, by making the most of the lovely flowers and foliage that will be available.

As well as vases of cut flowers and foliage, you can also make a living display of plants, which looks especially effective when arranged in a deep window sill, as shown in the photograph on the facing page. I chose a mixture of garden plants, including pansies, freesias, ivies, forsythia and various other plants, with moss and pebbles to hide their soil. These plants can be taken out of the garden (or bought from a nursery and replanted in the garden afterwards) and planted in individual pots. Cover the window sill with a thick sheet of plastic to prevent any soil or moisture leaching through, then arrange the plants, in their pots, on the plastic. Pieces of bark, twisted stems or roots can also be incorporated into the display to make it more interesting. Place the tallest plants at the back of the display, and trail some small plants, such as ivy, over the front of the window sill to soften the edge and hide any pieces of plastic that might otherwise be visible. Then cover the tops and sides of the pots with a blanket of moss, arranging it into tendrils at the front and holding it in place with a few pebbles. You could create this arrangement in a child's bedroom or playroom, in your living room or for a friend as an Easter present. For Easter Sunday itself, you could hide chocolate eggs or bunnies amid the foliage for an Easter egg

Facing page *A deep window sill filled with plants is an unusual but charming Easter decoration.* Over page *This sweetly-scented basket of yellow and white flowers would get any day off to a good start.*

hunt with a difference.

If you do not have enough small flowering plants in your garden, cover the window sill with the plastic sheeting and a few plants in pots, as before, then place a quarter of a block of wet oasis on the sheet and arrange in it a selection of cut flowers and foliage. This will give you the added colour and varying shapes you need to make the arrangement look alive.

All too often breakfast is rather a hurried affair, but during the Easter break you have the perfect opportunity to start the day in a leisurely and relaxed way. Get out your favourite china, make a special effort to prepare some delicious breakfast food and give the table the perfect finishing touch with a pretty arrangement of scented spring flowers. Freesias and narcissi are good choices because they are particularly fragrant and delicate-looking.

For my breakfast table display I arranged 'Cheer' narcissi, yellow parrot tulips, 'Connecticut King' lilies, white freesias and eucalyptus in a broom basket. The lilies contrast dramatically with the narcissi and the fatness of the tulips, and the white freesias make the arrangement look crisp and fresh, thereby accentuating the yellows and creams. If you removed the white from the arrangement, it would become rather dull and lifeless and equally, if you took out the cream, the remaining flowers would form too sharp and stark a contrast. The eucalyptus was a natural choice because it is soft and dark green, and lime green would have been too similar in colour to the rest of the foliage.

In this arrangement, I lined the basket with thick plastic and then filled it with wet oasis, as it is virtually impossible to find a container to fit the exact shape of the basket you wish to use. Since both the narcissi and tulips have rather fat and weak stems, you should use a pencil or similar-shaped object to drill the holes in the oasis before inserting the flowers. Do this first, then arrange the other flowers and foliage afterwards.

As an alternative, if you don't mind how long the arrangement lasts, you can wire the stems of the narcissi and tulips, but nevertheless they should still be arranged before the other flowers and foliage. As a general rule, it is always wise to arrange the fattest-stemmed flowers and foliage first, as they can take up a great deal of room in the oasis or wire netting.

In a rather different vein and style is the bird's nest arrangement, which can also be placed on a deep window sill. Instead of using plants you could find some interesting-looking twigs to create the basic shape, and use lots of bark to make an intriguing foreground. I used moss to soften the hard lines of the bark and to camouflage the mechanics.

To make this arrangement, place a block of oasis on a piece of plastic sheeting, insert the branches first and then add either fresh flowers and foliage (in which case the oasis should have been well-soaked in water first) or artificial material. However, you may be able to find some blossom that could be used instead of the twigs. In this particular display, I used twisted willow, artificial plums and a few other artificial flowers, then added some quails' eggs and artificial dragonflies. To make the nest, use a small piece of wire netting for the basic frame, then cover it with moss, holding it in place with reel wire. You could then fill the nest with chocolate eggs if you wished. However, you must make sure that you secure the nest firmly on to the branches, and that it is stable.

An arrangement like this could also be placed against a blank wall and then lit at night in such a way that the twisted willow throws attractive shadows on the wall. Should you wish, you could also arrange a few nightlights amidst the bark, but you must then ensure that you do not leave them unattended.

Clever lighting enhances the effectiveness of this bird's nest arrangement and makes it an intriguing Easter decoration.

CHRISTMAS

The exuberance of Christmas decorations gives every flower arranger wonderful scope, whether one adheres to the traditional colours of red and green, or uses them as a springboard for a host of different and exciting designs. As well as the abundance of foliage that can be used and the various flowers that are available at this time of year, you can also incorporate fruits, vegetables, nuts and other items traditionally associated with Christmas, such as glass baubles, tiny toys, trinkets and sweets. The more you let your imagination run riot, the more unusual and innovative the ideas you will have. If you run short of inspiration, the words of a Christmas carol or story, or perhaps a particular tradition, may be just the spur you need to create some interesting arrangements.

Mantelpieces are often the focal points of rooms, making them ideal decorative areas at Christmas. If you don't want to display cards along the mantel, you can use plenty of foliage, fruits, nuts, candles, baubles or other Christmas decorations instead.

If you are using foliage, unless you will want to take down your decorations shortly after Christmas, or are prepared to renew them halfway through the festive season, you should choose material that will last well and not wilt or drop its leaves. In this chapter you will see photographs of a few of my ideas for decorating fireplaces and tables, all of which can be adapted for other surfaces and purposes with a little thought.

My swagged fireplace consists of one horizontal and two vertical swags, with church candles on the mantel and a large red and green arrangement of flowers and foliage in the grate. The swags were made from holly, blue pine, nuts and cones, and finished with large bows of wire-edged burgundy ribbon. They can either be suspended from nails hammered into the surround or, if you have the right type of fireplace, they can be attached with wires.

If you are inexperienced at it, making one swag could take you a good three hours, so do leave plenty of time to complete the arrangement. Wire all the nuts, cones, pine and holly on to 0.71mm (22 gauge) wire and, starting from the bottom, work upwards. The swag lying across the mantelpiece itself is made from the same materials as the vertical ones, but includes tangerines as well. Two church candles placed on the mantelpiece are a dramatic finishing touch, and I twisted trails of ivy around them to incorporate them with the rest of the arrangement.

The fireplace arrangement used oasis placed in a large heavy china bowl – a big old-fashioned mixing bowl would be perfect. This is to enable you to fit at least three blocks of wet oasis into the bowl to give it weight and stability, as most of the flowers will be leaning forwards out of the fireplace. In this arrangement, I used green holly, grey eucalyptus, a little blue pine, red gerberas, various types of pine cone and a few shiny red apples lying on the floor. If you don't have enough red flowers, you could use some red bows made from the same ribbon as that used to tie the swags to the fireplace. If you do not have any flowers at all, you could use such plants as poinsettia, foliage with colour or berries, or both, if possible. If you do use poinsettias, remove each plant from its pot, check that the root ball is moist, then wrap it tightly in plastic. Insert two thin bamboo or green garden sticks into the bottom of each root ball and use these to anchor the poinsettias in place in the oasis.

A very different effect can be obtained using clever lighting and lots of imagination. If you wish to recreate my frosty Christmas arrangement, which uses a mirror as part of the decoration, you should first find some contorted pieces of lichen-encrusted twigs, or other twigs that are equally interesting in

Facing page *The classic Christmas colours of red and green give this fireplace a very warm, traditional look.* Over page *As a complete contrast, this fireplace has been decorated for an evocative, frosted effect.*

shape. Then put a large sheet of plastic on a garage or cement floor, spread out the twigs and, working with each one in turn, spray with glue and immediately sprinkle silver or frosted glitter all over it. Leave to dry for a couple of seconds then remove from the spraying area and spray the next twig. While doing this you should ensure that your working area is adequately ventilated. Once all the sprayed and glittered twigs are dry, choose about seven of the most interesting and gnarled pieces and wire them together into the same shape as the mirror that you will be using. Place the twig arrangement on the mirror and bind the top twigs with the wire or hook that attaches the mirror to the wall, making sure that it is quite safe and secure. Choose a piece of silk lining fabric, about 5m (5½yd) long and preferably grey in colour, then twine this in and out of the twigs. Once you have done this, add some more twigs until you achieve a full and dramatic effect.

Do make sure that you don't completely cover the mirror itself in fabric and twigs, otherwise its impact will be lost. Then either hang glass baubles or teardrop glass balls from the extending branches. To increase the atmospheric effect, I made a few cobwebs from reel wire, then covered them with glue and glitter as before.

The candles sit in small round oasis dishes, made from white plastic. First, cut a hole, slightly smaller than the diameter of the candle, out of half a block of wet oasis. Once you have done this, insert the candle into the hole (do so in the kitchen, as a lot of water will escape from the oasis). Now secure the oasis to the dish with thick white oasis tape and cover the mound of oasis with damp lichen moss. To secure it use 5-cm (2-in) pins of black wire inserted through the moss into the oasis, ensuring

Facing page *Easily and quickly made, an Advent ring is an ideal table decoration. Over page Pyramids of fruit and nuts make a colourful display for a mantelpiece at Christmas.*

that the pins do not show. Arrange seven or so twigs in the oasis, making sure that there are not too many long twigs sticking out that could catch people as they walk past. Hang small glass baubles or teardrop balls from the branches, especially from the extremities. This arrangement will look lovely when the candles are lit, but I must stress that they should not be left burning when unattended, nor allowed to burn too low, so ensure you have plenty of spares.

Advent rings are also traditional Christmas features (*see p 103*), and consist of four candles arranged amidst a bed of foliage. One candle is lit on each successive Sunday in Advent, until all four of them are burning brightly by the time Christmas arrives. As well as being a lovely decoration in its own right, especially when placed in the centre of a table, an Advent ring helps impatient children mark off the seemingly endless weeks until Christmas!

I made my Advent ring from blue pine, walnuts, pine cones and red apples, with red candles and tiny silver balls for decoration. You can also use tangerines or any other sorts of fruit and nuts that are available, and even little presents or plastic-wrapped sweets. As there is a hole in the middle of the ring, you could fill it with foil-wrapped chocolates, liqueur chocolates, more nuts, petit fours, German ginger biscuits or pieces of shortbread.

The basis of the arrangement is an oasis ring, which can be bought ready-made and should be soaked in water before using. Start the ring by fitting the candles into their holders, then inserting the points of the holders into the oasis at regular intervals. Strip the lower 5cm (2in) of needles from each stem of blue pine then push them into the oasis so that they all face in the same direction and lie as flat to the ring as possible. Wire the apples through their bottoms with 1.25mm (18 gauge) wire, bend the wires to form pins and cut them until they only protrude about 5–7.5cm (2–3in) from the apples, then position them around the Advent ring. Push

1.25mm (18 gauge) wire through the star at the bottom of each walnut, trim the wire as before and insert in the oasis. The cones used here still had their own stems, with which they were pushed into the oasis, but if the stems on yours have been removed, you will have to attach the pine cones to the oasis with 0.71mm (22 gauge) wire. Wrap the wire around the lowest open kernels, twist it on to itself and then pull the two pieces of wire down towards the base of the cone and trim, before pushing into the oasis. Cluster together bunches of the silver balls and then insert them in the oasis. You should replace the candles whenever they burn down, and never leave them burning unattended, as they could easily become fire hazards.

For a very different style of Christmas decoration, you can arrange small pyramids made from fruits and nuts on either side of the mantelpiece (*see pp 104–5*). As well as being full of differing colours and textures, they are also fairly easy to make. Choose a pair of matching containers, then make two pyramids of oasis covered in wire netting and wire them securely on to the bowls. In this case, I wired the oasis on to the handles of the bowls.

You can use any combination of fruits and nuts, as long as you choose varying sizes and colours. Here, I used apples, walnuts, grapes, radishes, artificial plums and lichen moss. You should cut all the apples in half widthways, to stop them protruding too far. This will also give you the basic pattern to follow, so arrange these up the pyramid first. When wiring walnuts, you should push the wire through the star at the bottom of each walnut. Some nuts are not as easy to work with, and you may have to drill a hole in them or, when working with brazil nuts, slice off their bottoms before wiring. If using small or tender fruits and vegetables,

Although this table decoration is mainly red and green in colour, the pink roses completely alter its impact, lending it a modern, fresh feeling.

such as grapes and radishes, you should string them together with button thread, then arrange them around the pyramids and secure in place with small wire pins. Once all the fruit has been arranged on the pyramid, you can fill in the gaps with damp lichen moss.

Departing from the classic decorations can make a refreshing change at Christmas (*see p 107*), and if your home is very modern a traditional arrangement may even look out of place. With this in mind, I created a table arrangement which gives a different dimension to the usual Christmas colours of red and green, using blue pine, berried ivy and pinky-blue 'Little Silver' and rich velvety-red roses, both of which are very strongly scented. You can, of course, use other foliage and flowers instead if they are more easily available.

This arrangement is made on a low black oasis tray, with one complete block of oasis taped in place. The candles should be placed in their holders and then inserted in the oasis before the foliage and flowers are positioned. There is no need for wiring in this arrangement, as all the stems can be pushed into the oasis as they are, although when using blue pine you should strip the needles from the lower 5cm (2in) of stem so that they will slide easily into the oasis.

Make a basic shape with the blue pine and berried ivy. As you are using rather round, solid flower shapes, be very careful not to let them look like one heavy mass but instead let each rose have its own space by pushing some in quite close to the oasis and arranging others in various heights until you achieve a pleasing effect.

This arrangement will last for between two to three days if it is left in a cool place when not in use. You will also have to keep the oasis wet and frequently spray the roses with water. As with all other arrangements incorporating candles, you must keep a close eye on them when lit, and have a ready supply of fresh candles to hand so that you can replace them whenever they burn down low.

If you want to introduce a note of drama into your Christmas decorations, an enormous bowl of striking flowers placed on a pedestal will help create the desired effect. It would look marvellous if placed in a large hallway, and will help to bring a living room to life. I chose eucalyptus, peachy-orange spray chrysanthemums, eucomis, amaryllis, yellow lilies, rusty Singapore orchids, ivy and various other foliages. If you feel that these are rather too many flowers at a time when they may be expensive in the shops or simply unavailable in the garden, you can create the same size of arrangement using various pines, variegated holly, berried holly, berried cotoneaster, mistletoe and perhaps even some attractive foliage from the garden. The arrangement may not then look as bright and colourful but it will be just as beautiful and dramatic. If you still feel that you would like to use some sort of red flower, you could always choose poinsettias, but first you must remember to remove each root ball from its pot, make sure it is moist and then wrap it in plastic before incorporating it into the arrangement.

This arrangement was created in a large brown bowl with wire netting and tubes. I didn't want to use oasis because the stems of the amaryllis are large and rather weak so that it is not possible to push them into the oasis without breaking them. Before using the cut amaryllis, you should insert a thin green garden stick or bamboo pole through the centre of the stem until it touches the flower head, then cut the stick so that no more than 7.5cm (3in) protrudes from the bottom of the stem. This will stop the natural stem bending under the weight of the amaryllis flowers once they have fully opened. Set up the bowl and tubes (*see pp 24–5*), then place the longest stem of

The strong colours of the flowers in this pedestal arrangement give it added impact and would help brighten up any room.

foliage three-quarters of the way back behind the tubes. This piece should be just slightly taller than anything else, but please don't leave it standing on its own! Finish arranging the foliage skeleton, then position the amaryllis as they are the biggest-stemmed flowers in the arrangement. Next, arrange the chrysanthemums, eucomis, lilies, orchids and then finally you can add the ivy.

For many people, despite their good intentions to the contrary, Christmas is usually a time of gastronomic excess. As a result, I believe that the arrival of the new year calls for a different style of decoration that is less heavy and opulent. You can still keep most of your Christmas decorations in place, but you may wish to replace some with lighter, crisper and brighter designs when ushering in the new year.

If you will be throwing a buffet party, decorating the food tables with arrangements composed of sharp greens and crisp whites will revive all but the most jaded of palates. I made a pair of very small fruit and flower pyramids, consisting mainly of green grapes and apples, *Euphorbia marginata*, eucalyptus and white freesias, which I chose especially for their wonderful scent. Once again, you should not eat any of the fruit used in the pyramid, as it is attached to the oasis with wires. I made these pyramids using bowls that were about 15cm (6in) in diameter, with one block of oasis per pyramid, trimmed to a conical shape, covered with wire netting and then secured to the bowls with silver reel wire.

If you are lucky enough to have snowdrops growing in your garden, you could fill three or five low bowls with the snowdrops and group them in the centre of the table. This will look stunning and create a talking point for your guests, giving them a hint of the spring to come.

As an alternative to flowers, a profusion of fresh fruit or large bowls of mixed fruits and nuts can be used for display, as well as eating, purposes. Alternatively, on two corners of the table, you can place mounds of fruit, with trails of grapes and ivy to follow, yet soften, the lines of the table. When displaying the food on dishes, you can decorate the individual plates with ivy leaves and small clumps of fruit. This always makes the food look extra special and more appetising. Crudités and bowls of mixed olives also help to give colour to a buffet table.

Crisp, light and fresh floral arrangements to celebrate the new year can come as a welcome relief after the richness and opulence of Christmas decorations.

New Home Flowers

Moving house can be an extremely traumatic affair – not only can one spend weeks searching for the right property, negotiating leases and prices, and picking one's way through a minefield of potential problems, but even when one has actually moved there can be many chores to tackle or upheavals to contend with while the builders take over or you begin the mammoth task of decorating. So, not only can a large vase of lovely flowers turn a bare room into an oasis of beauty but it can also act as a considerable tonic for the newcomers themselves.

One such arrangement that would make an ideal present to give to someone who has just moved into a new home is shown in the photograph on the facing page. The elegant lines of the lily vase, and the profusion of different shapes, textures and colours of the flowers and foliage, mean that it looks marvellous whether sitting on a packing case or standing on the floor.

When selecting the flowers for this type of vase, try to choose ones that have relatively thin stems if you wish to create a full effect, otherwise the slender neck of the vase will soon be filled although you may have a meagre-looking arrangement. I used blossom, 'Darling' roses, lilac, bouvardia, euphorbia, trailing ivy and large pink lilies. There was no need for either wire netting or oasis, because once I had positioned about five stems of blossom, they filled the vase enough to support the other flowers. I then added the lilac, followed by the lilies, and filled in the spaces with the roses, bouvardia and euphorbia, leaving the ivy until last.

In a design of this type it is essential to use ivy or trailing jasmine to balance the width of the flowers above the vase. This arrangement does need a lot of tendering as the volume of water is not great, and you will find that you have to top up the vase at least twice a day. If you look closely at the photograph, you will see that the stems do not extend far into the vase, because the neck is so narrow; the foliage has been trailed down to hide the stems that would otherwise be visible in the glass neck.

It is important to use flowers as large as these lilies and lilac to give the arrangement form. At Veevers Carter Flowers we have often created similar arrangements using just lilies and ivy, which are very impressive but also, because of the cost of the lilies, very expensive. The elegant shape of this vase means that you will find that even with a few stems of foliage or blossom, or virtually any tall and flowing foliage or flower, you will create a design that looks quite stunning.

Vases of this type are often used as table arrangements for large parties held in big halls, as they give a much more dramatic first impression than a row of low flower arrangements, and when they are crammed to overflowing with flowers they create a most sumptuous atmosphere.

Filling a fish bowl with flowers is another lovely way to welcome someone into their new home, but you should be very careful in your handling of the bowl itself. Firstly, you should always arrange flowers in a fish bowl *in situ*, as it is extremely heavy when full of water. It is also very difficult to carry, and if you try to transport the bowl by holding it anywhere other than the sides, the glass may shatter because of its thinness.

This is a large full arrangement, intended to sit on a chest or table, either in the centre of the room or to one side. We used rusty Singapore orchids, yellow lilies, 'Golden Shower' orchids, 'Lovely Girl' and 'Bahama' roses, red bouvardia, spray chrysanthemums, alstroemeria and eucalyptus. Rather than arrange the flowers in oasis, which would have been visible through the glass, I taped a double layer of wire netting to the top of the vase. To create the arrangement, position the foliage first, followed by the chrysanthemums, lilies, alstroemeria, roses, bouvardia and

The long, clean lines of this lily vase help make any arrangement, whether lavish or simple, a success.

orchids. Train the foliage down over the sides of the fish bowl to hide the netting, and to soften the outline of the bowl.

Because of the rounded shape of the fish bowl, I feel that the flowers should reflect the same sort of shape. The colours used in this arrangement were obviously chosen to blend in with the curtains, but if you look closely you will notice that only the orangey-red colours in the fabric have been picked out in the arrangement, while the yellows and creams complement but do not reflect the curtains. If you examine the photograph of the winter dried flower arrangement (*see p 128*), you will see the difference in effect when the flowers are virtually the same colours as the background.

The main problem in using glass is that the dirty water shows up immediately, which is no bad thing as it will remind you to change it whenever necessary. Although it looks like an impossible job to remove the water from this vase, all you have to do is loosen the tape which holds the netting in place, pick the flowers just above the wire

netting out of the vase and get someone to hold them while you change the water. To put them back, the person who is helping you should hold the bunch over the mouth of the vase while you very gently pull the stems together and ease them back into the water. You will find that the flowers should now balance themselves well enough for you not to have to retape the netting. If you wish to do so, however, you will have to use new tape, as the old will not stick, and ensure that the sides of the vase are dry.

Of course, it isn't always appropriate to welcome people into their new home with a large, exotic or exuberant flower arrangement. Instead, a small container of old-fashioned or classic garden flowers may be more suitable, especially for someone who is moving into a cottage or rustic house in the country. You could, perhaps, buy a

Above *This basket arrangement of Rosa rubrifolia leaves, copper beech, spurge, red roses and pink phlox would make an ideal moving-in present.* Facing page *A fish bowl is a simple but effective vase.*

large milk jug or old vase, and then fill it with suitable flowers, making a lovely homely present.

I created a very simple arrangement that can be gathered together in the hand before being placed in the vase or jug and allowed to fall into position. If you wish to reproduce this sort of effect it is always a good idea to choose some flowers that have plenty of branches to give support to the single-stemmed ones. I used aquilegia, laurustinus, sweet william, wax flower and white roses for this relaxed and comfortable arrangement.

Just as you don't always have to work with masses of flowers, neither do you need to use expensive, modern or unusual vases, as the flowers will look good in virtually any container. On this window sill I filled three jam jars with daisy chrysanthemums, September flower, anemones, spray carnations, wax flower, laurustinus, 'Bahama' roses and a mixture of herbs.

If you have created a large arrangement and found, a few days later, that most of it has died, you may be able to salvage a few flowers and make them up into an informal, small arrangement. Equally, if you have just moved into a new property you may be able to pick a few flowers from the garden to brighten up the house while you arrange your belongings.

In addition to their culinary uses, herbs make good foliage or can form an arrangement in their own right. Even if you intend to use them for cooking, there is nothing to stop you arranging a few herbs attractively before they are used and, for example, you could fill a jar with mint in the summer.

When arranging flowers it is important to think small as well as large. Here, these informal collections of garden flowers and herbs are enhanced by being arranged in jam jars and jugs.

OUTDOOR PARTIES

I always think there is something very special about holding a party out of doors – if the weather is kind, of course! The surroundings often help to make the party more relaxed and informal, and weddings can be particularly suited to outdoor settings.

If you are planning to hold a party outside, naturally the more flowers and interesting foliage that are already growing in the proposed area, the fewer arrangements you will need to create. If you will be holding the party in your own garden and have a lot of shrubs but not many flowers, you can easily create the illusion of plenty of growing flowers. Simply bury bottles filled with water in the ground, leaving their necks just protruding above the earth, and then fill them with such straight-stemmed flowers as phlox, delphiniums or lilies, remembering to include some of their foliage as well. You will gain a much more realistic effect if you bury groups of five or seven bottles in close proximity so that the flowers resemble a bush rather than just single stems.

When arranging your garden for a party it is very important not to leave too much open space, otherwise the first guests in particular will feel very exposed and self-conscious, and be reluctant to move away from the sides of the garden into the middle, thereby creating an uneasy atmosphere. You could also arrange little groups of tables and chairs in various parts of the garden, or shade a particularly sunny spot with a large and attractive umbrella.

One lovely decoration in any garden is a stone urn filled with flowers and foliage. If you already have some urns in your garden, you could either fill them with flowering plants or create large flower arrangements inside them. Whichever option you choose,

Try to make use of existing decorative features in the garden. Over page *If the garden is well stocked with flowers and shrubs you will not have to provide many other decorations.*

you should ensure that the urns are well-secured in case someone knocks against them or a gust of wind upsets them. If you want to buy some urns especially for your party, ideally you should do so several months in advance, and paint them with natural yoghurt to encourage the growth of mould and moss. This stops them looking obviously newly-bought, and with luck they will look as if they have been in your garden for years by the time of the party. Stone urns can be used inside as well as out, and I think they look especially attractive in a church or old hall.

To decorate the urn shown in the photograph on page 119 I filled it with cow parsley, delphiniums, rubrum lilies and phlox. As stone is porous, I had to give the urn a waterproof lining, and so filled a plastic bowl with blocks of wet oasis before wiring some wire netting over the top of the bowl. I then placed the bowl inside the urn and wired the two together.

Placing a large umbrella in the centre of an empty lawn creates a strong focal point and also brings people into the middle of the garden, especially if you group tables or decorative chairs around it. Arranging garlands of flowers around its edge will make the umbrella look more attractive and interesting. To do this, make rolls of wire netting, containing oasis blocks, as you would for an archway (*see p 29*), ensuring that each one is long enough to stretch from one spoke to the next. Firmly wire the ends of each roll to the spokes and then position the flowers. I used wild gypsophila, white campanulas, Doris pinks, *Alchemilla mollis* and lavender sweet peas, to give a very pretty, summery and rather frothy effect.

Very often the base of the umbrella is rather unattractive, but it can easily be transformed with some foliage and flowers. I placed blocks of wet oasis around the base, covered them with wire netting and then arranged plenty of grasses and a few stems of phlox to hide the base and give an informal effect. Bun moss and pieces of bark will cover up any mechanics that are left exposed, and also help to create additional interest.

Obelisks are rather unusual garden decorations, and therefore can create a stunning impact at parties, especially if they are used to frame an entrance, and to form an effective link between one part of the garden and another, inviting the guests to wander about at will. Normally, obelisks are free-standing and rest on top of boxes, and are usually planted with ivy, roses or other trailing plants. However, they can easily be detached from their boxes if you want to place them on an existing plinth, to create the type of effect shown in the photograph on the facing page. Here, I wired spider plants (chlorophytum) through the trellis work and covered their pots with sphagnum moss. Alternatively, you could fill the obelisk with small posies of flowers, create a flower arrangement in the centre, or even leave them plain, with just a little trailing ivy to give a decorative effect. Your choice of flowers or plants will be determined, of course, by the nature of the party and the season in which it takes place.

In addition to any existing trees in the garden, you can also create your own rose trees that resemble stylised standard rose bushes. Like obelisks, they look very attractive arranged by the walkway leading to an entrance or used to frame a special feature in the garden. You can make them in any size, although I would strongly suggest that if they are more than 1.2m (4ft) high they should be secured to a wall or some other permanent and strong structure, to prevent any danger of their toppling over. I used a mixture of roses for the trees shown in the photograph on pages 124–5, with *Alchemilla mollis* arranged in the pot to cover the mechanics (*see p 32*), although

Filling an obelisk with spider plants creates added architectural interest and provides a link between one area of the garden and another. Over page *Rose trees and wall arrangements give colour and draw the eye to this stone seat and wall.*

you could use moss instead. Unfortunately, these trees do not last very long and therefore must be made on the day of the party.

Bare walls are sometimes decorative features in their own right, but you can increase their attractiveness with trays of flowers that are placed on top of the wall or on the ground close by. To make a wall arrangement, wire or tape a block of oasis on to an oasis tray, then create the arrangement *in situ*. You can then let the flowers and foliage trail if they are to be placed on the wall, or make the arrangement taller and wider if it is to be on the ground.

Amongst the flowers suitable for wall and ground decorations are cornflowers, roses, phlox and alchemilla. If time and space allow, you could have trays of flowers running all along the top of the wall, or along the bottom rather like a herbaceous border if one doesn't already exist. You could even range them along both the top and bottom of the wall, with long trails of jasmine, roses or ivy running from the top arrangements down to the bottom ones to virtually cover the wall. This is especially suitable if the wall itself is unattractive, past its best or broken in places.

If the wall arrangements will be more than 45cm (18in) tall, I suggest that you use a plastic trough, rather than an oasis tray, as it will be safer and more stable. For added security you should wire the trays or troughs to masonry nails that you have hammered into the wall. If the wall is composed of a row of pillars, nails will not be necessary as you will be able to thread wire through the pillars instead. Better safe than sorry!

A garlanded umbrella not only looks pretty but can also provide some much-needed shade in hot weather.

INDOOR PARTIES

Gone are the days when dried flowers were available in two colours only – cream and brown. With the new drying methods you do not have to suffer either the dull, natural yet boring colours, or the extraordinarily vivid shades of dyed dried flowers. You can make the flowers dry to virtually the colour of the fresh ones and with the use of glycerined eucalyptus you can create some very lively and bright floral decorations.

In my winter arrangement, I used solidaster, delphiniums, red and yellow roses, blue eucalyptus and nigella, using brown oasis covered in sphagnum moss to cover the oasis. If your dried flower stems are not long enough, you can wire them on to green garden sticks, using 0.71mm (22 gauge) black wire. However, you must ensure that your mechanics do not show in the finished result.

For an elegant cocktail or dinner party, I think that a fireplace arrangement of cool greens, whites and greys creates exactly the right impression of sophistication yet originality. I chose longiflorum lilies, blossom, eucalyptus, cow parsley and giant hogweed, so that the lime green and grey of the eucalyptus would set off the strong pure white of the lilies, which would then be softened by the delicate quality of the cow parsley. You may feel slightly daunted by the apparent expense of using longiflorum lilies, but you only need three to five stems to fill a relatively large arrangement. However, I do feel that you should

Facing page *If it is difficult to find a variety of interesting flowers in the winter, you could make a permanent arrangement of dried flowers and foliage instead.* Below *The luminous quality of the longiflorum lilies, cow parsley and giant hogweed makes them stand out from their black surround.*

complement the lilies with light and pretty foliage rather than using, as many people seem to, somewhat heavy and dark green leaves, which to me make the lilies look extremely funereal. When creating this arrangement, use wire netting and a china trough of water, as this will ensure the cow parsley and giant hogweed stay fresh for as long as possible – they would not be able to drink freely if inserted in oasis.

Wall plaques are much easier to make than they appear, and yet they lend a sense of drama and occasion to any room in which they are displayed. They can take the place of pictures on a wall for a party, be hung on the walls of a marquee or even placed on a door, and in addition to being made from fresh flowers, as in the photograph on the facing page, they can also be made from dried or silk flowers for a permanent plaque. Here, I used lilac, cow parsley, *Euphorbia marginata*, tuberoses, eucalyptus, 'Little Silver' roses, champagne roses and ornamental pineapples for an arrangement that is full of surprises.

Using artificial flowers would enable you to arrange the plaque at your leisure, and in fact I would recommend practising with dried or silk flowers before attempting to use fresh ones, which have to be positioned quickly and accurately.

To make the arrangement, wrap a block of wet oasis in wire netting, securing the ends together, and then fill it with the flowers. I arranged the pineapples first, using their stems to hold them in place, followed by the eucalyptus, *Euphorbia marginata*, cow parsley, lilac, tuberoses and finally the roses. This arrangement was suspended in mid-air for a purely photographic effect but it is not advisable, because these plaques need to be stabilised. Instead, if you wish to make a hanging arrangement you should use a wire hanging basket, filled with oasis and lined with moss and black plastic to give a much safer and more satisfactory effect.

If you have ever wondered what to do with all your dying tulips or roses, making pot-pourri could be the perfect answer. Pull off all the petals when the flowers are over but before they turn brown, spread them thinly over baking sheets and leave in an airing cupboard for a week or so until they are completely dry, then add some orris root (this 'fixes' the scent) and essential oils of your choice, mix well and store in an airtight container for six weeks, shaking well on alternate days. The pot-pourri shown in the photograph on page 132 was made from the petals of various roses and parrot tulips, both striped and plain, to give added colour, shape and interest.

Pot-pourri makes a marvellous decoration, whether it is placed in a glass fish bowl as we have shown in the photograph, in a low Chinese dish or any other attractive container of your choice. It also makes an excellent present for Christmas or any other occasion and it is so much more original and special if you make it yourself.

Hallowe'en is one time of year when you can really let your imagination run riot when planning the arrangements for a party. There is such scope for unusual decorations, and the clever use of colours, shapes and textures will help you to create the right atmosphere of mystery, suspense and excitement.

Some effects, of course, are much more involved and complicated than others, and you may only want to make a table arrangement or floral decoration. However, if you are feeling adventurous, you could turn a complete room into a witches' coven or a similarly spine-chilling setting (*see pp 134–5*). Although you may not wish to create exactly the same effect, you should be able to adapt it for use during a party in your own home.

I used a lot of sprayed cobwebs, dry ice, smoke machines and intricate lighting to give the effect shown in the photograph.

If properly lit and made with stunning or unusual flowers, a wall plaque can form a good talking point at a party.

The main structure was made from gnarled, moss- and lichen-covered branches, and I hung a very coarse netting over the ceiling to make it look foggy and mysterious. I used a real pumpkin for the lantern, carving an appropriate face out of it and placing a short candle inside.

You could create a similar effect by draping swags of white, grey and black

The delicate scents of home-made pot-pourri will gently pervade any room and remind you of sunny days even in the depths of winter. Facing page White lilies, stock and eucalyptus leaves make this arrangement look fresh and bright. Over page Hallowe'en is a marvellous opportunity to give full rein to your imagination when decorating a room for a party.

netting across the ceiling. To give the right moody atmosphere you could light the room with uplighters and shine a garden light through the window to cast reflections on to the ceiling. Atmosphere is all in a design like this, so look for anything that will create the right air of mystery. For example, I found two wooden elephants and fake stone boulders, but you could use gnarled tree roots, half-broken baskets and even old garden rakes which will all take on a completely new dimension once they are incorporated into this design.

Since Hallowe'en has always been a time for giving full rein to one's imagination, if you do throw a party you will find that everyone loves to dress up and, for people who have taken the trouble to look the part, it is worth creating an atmosphere that reflects their costumes and the overall sense of adventure. Don't forget background noises – you could record a tape of creaking doors, howling winds, moans and groans, trees tapping at window panes or low whispering voices. If you concealed the tape recorder at the back of the display, and then played the tape very softly, your guests would hear it in the distance and not know whether the strange sounds they were hearing were purely their imagination playing tricks or something much more real and disturbing. . . .

A less ambitious, but nonetheless equally effective, Hallowe'en display is a table arrangement (*see facing page*). Here, I used mushrooms, garlic, heather, 'Champagne' roses, small cabbage leaves, mixed green foliage, broccoli and an artificial dragonfly and lizard.

I placed the arrangement in a basket because it gave a more natural effect than a china or glass bowl would have done. Using vegetables in a table arrangement creates interest at a dinner party and enables you to use any vegetables you have to hand or growing in the garden, although for Hallowe'en ideally they should be greyish and of an interesting shape. For instance, if you were making a similar arrangement in

the summer, you could use courgettes (zucchini), tomatoes, radishes and other seasonal vegetables. It is not necessary to use flowers, but foliage is important, as it helps to soften and shape the arrangement.

The mushrooms and garlic should be wired with 1.25mm (18 gauge) stub wire so that they stand away from the basket and give an interesting variation in height. The basket itself can be filled with either wire netting or oasis, depending on the strength of the stems of foliage, and possibly flowers, used. Other than the cabbage leaves, the rest of the foliage should be small-leaved and light to counteract the heaviness of the vegetables. If you are using orange or red vegetables you will have to ensure that at least one of the types of foliage is similarly coloured, as this will make the completed arrangement come together. As you will notice, I used grey foliage to blend the white of the garlic with the grey of the mushrooms.

When creating the arrangement, you will find it easiest to position the vegetables first, and then the largest leaves (in this case, cabbage). After this, the broccoli and the rest of the foliage and flowers (if used) should be added. In my arrangement, the artificial dragonfly and lizard were added extras but they are not essential. However, if you have children, you should be able to borrow from them some plastic or rubber spiders, snakes or lizards to place in or around the arrangement.

If you are looking for a very dramatic way of welcoming people to a party, constructing a birch tree arch is one very effective idea, and will help put your guests into the right mood. For the arch shown in the photograph, I used stripped birch branches, decorated with maidenhair and Boston ferns, artificial ivy and grapes, moss, bark and a few interestingly gnarled branches. Ideally for a party you would

Garlic, mushrooms and an artificial lizard and dragonfly are the unexpected but effective finishing touches to this table arrangement.

make this arch going upstairs, along an entrance to a marquee or a corridor in a hall or private house.

Should you wish to make it yourself, I strongly suggest that you do so in a place where there are two firm sides or walls on which to secure the branches. Depending on the time of year, you could do well to use birch trees in leaf, the greenery and fullness of which would considerably reduce the amount of other foliage that would be needed.

To make the arch, you must first secure the trees in place. If you are working with solid walls, hammer in two rows of nails on either side, one row about 30cm (1ft) from the ground and the other one 1m (1yd) from the ground. Then rest a long bamboo pole on each set of nails and wire in place until it is very secure. You can then fit the branches behind each pole. If you are working in a marquee, you should be able to use the existing frame instead of the bamboo poles, and when constructing this arrangement up a set of stairs you can wire the branches on to the banisters or guard rail on one side and fix up the bamboo poles on the other. If you don't want to mark the walls, you can set the branches into long troughs of nylon reinforced plaster. Once dry, they can be disguised with layers of moss and ferns.

To form the arch, having threaded the trees behind the poles or marquee frames, bend the top branches so that they overlap in the centre, and then wire them together with 0.71mm (22 gauge) stub wires. Do make sure that the resulting arch will be high enough for the tallest guest to pass through easily and remember that, when you have finished, you must go along the inside of the tunnel and trim any loose or protruding branches – otherwise, they could easily catch in someone's eyes or pull at their clothes.

Alternative trees include willow, privet and any other light, flexible trees. Heavy laurels, however, would not be suitable. When using birch trees, threading light camellia branches through them will give density as well as create a very pretty effect. You could also use large branches of cherry blossom (but not branches from your best edible cherry trees) or something similar, but if using a flowering tree you must leave it as late as possible before assembling the arch as the branches will be out of water and the blossom will soon droop. Equally, the moist root balls of the ferns should be wrapped in plastic sheeting before being incorporated into the arrangement.

For a different, starry effect, you can thread fairy lights through the branches and wire bunches of plastic grapes on to them for added interest and richness. Fresh ivy can be substituted for artificial but I don't recommend using fresh grapes as people will pull at them or they may drop on to the floor and be squashed underfoot. It is important to consider the flooring, as covering the floor of the tunnel with moss may look interesting but it will not be appreciated when it is traipsed throughout the rest of the building or party area. If the floor is attractive you could consider leaving it unadorned.

If you are throwing a party and worried that a particular room, hallway or landing looks rather bare, a large pedestal of flowers will fill the space with colour and form, and is often far more effective than several smaller and less striking vases. This type of arrangement looks especially stunning if placed at the head or foot of some stairs, but do make sure that there is enough room for your guests to walk about without fear of upsetting the vase. Furthermore, if you are creating a large arrangement that will be set on the floor, you must ensure that the vase is stable and high enough to give plenty of space between it and the floor.

When illuminated with tiny fairy lights, these birch trees look like an enchanted forest, and makes a marvellously exciting entrance to a party or marquee.

In my arrangement, I used guelder roses, white lilac, yellow lilies, forsythia, white roses, trailing ivy, eucalyptus and white stock. The mixture of lime green, yellow and white is very spring-like and has a fresh feel.

To form the basis of the arrangement, roll lots of wire netting into a deep vase. Because of its depth, there should be no need to tape or wire the netting into the vase as it will stay in position of its own accord. If you want the arrangement to fit into a corner, you will achieve a much better effect if you can work *in situ*. As in any large arrangement, you should start at the back, placing the first stem as far back into the vase as possible, so that you can then arrange the flowers to fit the space perfectly. Rather than the arrangement sticking out from the wall at the back, you will have to ensure that you build a triangular-shaped back to the design.

This arrangement incorporates many varieties in shape as well as colour, and I used trailing ivy to soften the vase. If the hall is narrow you would be ill-advised to let the ivy trail out over the floor as someone is bound to trip over or stand on it, and this could even make the arrangement overbalance.

A perfect way to trim a staircase for a party is to drape garlands and posies of flowers along the banisters. However, you had better check first that the staircase is wide enough to allow guests to pass up and down without damaging the flowers. I used *Euphorbia marginata*, guelder roses, eucalyptus and roses to make the posies, with garlands of smilax to link them along the banisters. To make the posies, cover quarter blocks of oasis with wire netting and back with plastic (*see pp 20–1*), then wire them on to the banisters and arrange the flowers in position. You can then loop the smilax between the posies. As alternatives, you could make garlands from ivy or ribbons, and the posies could be made from gypsophila or cow parsley for weddings, or mistletoe for Christmas.

Another charming decoration for a stairway is to cover one side of the stair treads with pillows of flowers, which are in fact made from black oasis trays. Once they are all decorated, they look like a continuous line of flowers.

To make them, tape one block of oasis to each tray with oasis tape, then place one on each stair tread and arrange the flowers *in situ*. If this is not possible, then when arranging the flowers you should leave one end of the oasis flat and undecorated – in other words, cover the front, top and one side of the oasis. If the oasis trays will be lined up against a wall you should leave the two sides undecorated as well as the back.

As with the posies and garlands, you should first check that the stairs are wide enough to accommodate this sort of decoration. Generally, these decorated stair treads are only used for weddings, but of course you can make them for any occasion you wish.

When using flowers in this sort of situation they should be as strongly scented as possible (lily of the valley, narcissi and hyacinths are all ideal), so that the scent will float up to the passers-by and circulate throughout the house. We used cow parsley, sprays of coral roses, 'Bahama' roses, 'Cheer' narcissi, cream hyacinths, lily of the valley and laurustinus, which combined to create a wonderful perfume. If you put lily of the valley, narcissi, roses or cow parsley into oasis, they will not last as long as they would do in water and wire netting, so you should leave it as late as possible before arranging them and then spray them continuously. The flowers should last for about 12 hours, unless the building is extremely hot.

Don't neglect the stairs when decorating your house for a party. As well as placing a large pedestal or vase on the landing (facing page), you can decorate the banisters with posies and garlands (over page, left) or cover the stairs themselves with a continuous line of flowers (over page, right).